WESTERN PHILOSOPHY OF EDUCATION

G.R. SHARMA

ATLANTIC PUBLISHERS AND DISTRIBUTORS

Published by
ATLANTIC PUBLISHERS AND DISTRIBUTORS
B-2, Vishal Enclave, Opp. Rajouri Garden, New Delhi-110 027
Phones : 5413460, 5429987, 54466842

Sales Office
4215/1, Ansari Road, Darya Ganj, New Delhi-110 002
Phones : 3273880, 3285873, 3280451
Fax : 91-11-3285873
web : www.atlanticbooks.com
e-mail : info@atlanticbooks.com

ISBN 81-269-0135-7

Typeset at
APD Computer Graphics, Delhi
Printed in India at
Mehra Offset Press, Delhi

PREFACE

The present book, *Western Philosophy of Education,* has been particularly designed to study all the essentials of Western philosophy of education in brief and precise format. It seeks to serve the needs of the undergraduate and postgraduate students as an ideal textbook and a reference book for teachers.

There is a plethora of books on the "Western Philosophy of Education" but these can hardly meet the requirements of the students. Thus, an attempt has been made to make this work an ideal textbook on the subject.

Suggestions, if any, for the improvement of the book in the next edition will be gratefully acknowledged.

G.R. SHARMA

CONTENTS

1

PLATO
(427-347 B.C.)

Life of Plato

Plato was born in 427 B.C., the son of noble parents. According to tradition he first studied music, poetry, painting and philosophy with other masters and became a pupil of Socrates in 407 B.C., remaining with him until the latter's death in 399 B.C., when he accompanied the sorrowing Socrates to Megara. He is said to have travelled in Egypt and Asia Minor, to have visited Italy and the Pythogoreans in 388 B.C., and to have lived for a time at the court of Dioysius I, the tyrant of Syracuse, who became his enemy and sold him into slavery as prisoner of war; but all of these stories have been denied. He founded a school in the groves of Academus, the Academy, where he taught mathematics and the different branches of philosophy, by means of connected lectures and the dialogue. The story goes that he interrupted his work on two occasions in 367 B.C. and 361 B.C., by further visits to Syracuse, presumably in the hope of assisting in the realization of his ideal State, and that he was disappointed in this hope. His death occurred in 347 B.C.

The life of Plato can be divided into three ages. In the first age he received education from his great master Socrates besides some other minor teachers. He lived with Socrates for eight years and received instructions and ideas in different fields of human thought. After the death of Socrates, perturbed as he was, Plato went on his journey through Egypt, Cyrene, Italy and Cisely, etc.

For ten years he was roaming in different countries observing their ways of life, social and political structures and institutions and discussing with scholars of different countries. It was in this age that he planned his important dialogues. During this period Plato's thinking was generally centred around ideas, the universals. The dialogues written during this period do not exhibit much literary excellence. The important dialogues written during this period were Gorgias, Theatetus, Sophistes, Statemen and Parmendies.

After ten years of journey in different countries Plato's mind was almost settled. He now returned to Athens and started third and the most important age of his life. He established an institution known as Academy of Gymnasium. Here he started to live as a teacher, a mathematician and a philosopher. For forty years he educated hundreds of illustrious disciples and created dozens of dialogues up to his death at the age of eighty-two.

Works of Plato

It seems unlikely that all of Plato's works have come down to us. Of the writings transmitted under his name — thirty-five Dialogues, thirteen Letters — most of the Letters and all of the definitions are considered to be spurious, although it seems likely that several of the letters including the philosophically important seventh letter, are genuine.

Chronological Order of Works

Attempts have been made by many scholars to arrange the dialogues in chronological order. One method of ordering them employs the criterion of relative maturity of philosophical doctrine, but this method has produced very different ordering by different scholars. A method which has in recent years proven very useful is the ordering of the dialogues in accordance with stylometric vocabulary of considerations, adopting as a standard, the style, and vocabulary of the laws, which is universally accepted as the latest of the dialogues. Sir David Ross, after summarizing these stylistic and linguistic investigations suggests the following probable order of the Platonic dialogues :

(1) *First Period (before 389-388 B.C.)* : Charmides, Laches, Euthyphro, Hipias Major, and Meno.

(2) *Second Period (between 389-388 B.C. and 367-366 B.C.)* : Cratylus (date doubtful), Symposium (385 B.C. or later), Phaedo, *The Republic*, Phaedrus, Parmenids, Theaetetus (369 B.C. or later).

(3) *Third Period (between 367-366 B.C. and 361-360 B.C.)* : Sophistes, Politicus.

(4) *Fourth Period (after 361-360 B.C.)* : *The Laws* (Plato's Theory of Ideas, Ch. I).

This list does not include those of the earlier dialogues which throw little or no light on Plato's theory of ideas : The Apology, Crito, Lysis, Protagoras, Gorgias and Euthydemus.

Spurious Dialogues

Among the thirty-five dialogues, the following are now generally rejected as spurious : Alcibiades I and Alcibiades II, Epinomis, Anteras, Hippachus, Theages, Minos, Cleitphro, Io, and Menexenus. Many scholars have questioned the genuineness of Hippias Major.

COMPREHENSION OF PLATO'S THOUGHT

Philosophy began in wonder as well as in the urge for understanding of world enigma. Men everywhere realised that the sensual world is not the only world effective in their life. They, therefore, tried to rise from the sensuous world to reach the height of supra-sensuous. Thus, ancient philosophy in India as well as in Greece was essentially an attempt to rise from sensuous impure to non-sensuous pure thought. Plato's philosophy is an example of such an attempt and his attempt, though carried out thousands of years ago, still stands unbeaten. The theory of ideas has been the source of evolution of idealist school in Western philosophy. As knowledge in his days was inter-connected and comprehensive, Plato has discussed a wide variety of human problems including those of epistemology, metaphysics, psychology, social and political philosophy. In those ancient days even astronomy and physical sciences were very much connected with social sciences and philosophy. Therefore, one finds important references to even these in the writings of Plato. Thus, philosophy was considered as the knowledge of the essence, the substance, that by knowing which everything else can be known. The philosopher was in search of a key to understand the world enigma. His search was not for the particulars but for the universal behind the particulars. His enquiry was directed to a theory which could explain all the mystery of creation, its what, how and why? He looked inwards, outwards as well as upwards. He analysed psychological processes, wondered at the nature of creator and tried to understand the world around him. Thus, philosophical practice was a comprehensive process. It included every branch of knowledge, nay the whole of human life. The philosopher, therefore, was everywhere held in high esteem.

Plato's Heritage

In Greek thought Plato was not the first philosopher. Long before him, illustrious schools of philosophy, including great scholars, developed and contributed important ideas to various fields of knowledge. This can be labelled as pre-Socratic age which started from sixth century B.C. and went on up to the middle of the fifth century B.C. The advent of sophists marked the end of this period. Then came the Socratic age in Greek thought. Socrates argued with the sophists and showed the hollowness of their thinking. He condemned negative approach to human knowledge and presented positive ideas. He himself wrote nothing but only used to discuss with various persons. It was his illustrious disciple Plato who gave a literary presentation to the ideas of Socrates in his famous dialogues. These dialogues again, are the sources of Plato's thought. In fact, one can hardly distinguish between the thought of Socrates and Plato. Plato, as a humble disciple of his master, never claimed originality, but eulogised Socrates and his thought. After Plato Aristotle was an illustrious philosopher of the Socratic age in Greek thought. His death in 322 B.C. marked the end of Socratic age which can be rightly considered as the source of all Western human knowledge.

Plato's Originality

Thus, Plato's philosophy was influenced, besides the ideas of his master Socrates, by the Milesian idea of substance, the infinite of Anaxemander, the numbers of Pythagoras, the universal of Heraclitus, the essence of Parmenides, the dialectics of Empedocles, the human criteria of Protagoras and his own experience of contemporary social and political conditions. This, however, does not mean that Plato's thoughts were a mere summary or synthesis of the ideas of his predecessors. It is certainly to the credit of this great cosmopolitan philosopher of the world that he presented a synthetic philosophy which marks the apex of Greek thought. His thought influenced almost all the social sciences particularly sociology and political science. In philosophy it had been the source of almost all great movements, of which some followed his principles while other criticised them. Even the German philosopher Immanual Kant, who made a Copernican revolution in the field of philosophy, owed much to Platonic thought.

Classification of Plato's Thought

Plato's philosophy has been divided into three classes — Dialectic, Physics and Ethics. Of these, Dialectic has been considered to be the most important in the field of philosophy while ethics has influenced sociology, political science, education, economics and all the fields of humanities. Dialectic includes his theory of ideas and epistemology. Physics includes his conceptions about the physical world and his views concerning psychology. Ethics includes Plato's ideas concerning individual life, the social life, the political life, the international relations, peace and war and the realisation of an ideal state.

With the sophist predecessors about the fourth or the third century before the Christian era, a new school of teaching came into being in Greece. The enlargement of the intellectual horizon resulting from the unrest that ensued demanded a class of men who could impart quickly every kind of knowledge. All sorts of conditions were pressed into the service of education and classed under the general title 'Sophist' to satisfy this demand.

Sophist Educators

The teaching of the sophists was unsystematic. It was also limited to the few who could pay for it. Socrates said, "As for myself, I am the first to confess that I have never had a teacher; although I have always from my earliest youth desired to have one. But I am too poor to give money to the sophists, who are the only professors of moral improvement."[1] As they accepted payment for their services there was a certain prejudice against the sophists, for this enabled those who could afford their instruction to acquire a definite superiority over their fellow-citizens. The popular attitude towards them may be inferred from the violent outburst of indignations with which Anytus received the suggestion of Socrates that Meno should go to the sophists for his education. "The young men," says Anytus, "who gave their money to them (the sophists) were out of their minds, and their relations and guardians who entrusted them to their care were still more out of their minds, and most of all the cities which allowed them to come in and did not drive them out, citizen or stranger alike.... Neither I nor any of my belongings has ever had, nor would I suffer them to have, anything to do with them."[2]

Objectives of Greek Education

The prejudice against the sophists was intensified by the fact that they degraded knowledge by making direct utility its aim. Education was with the Greeks a training for leisure, not for a livelihood. It is asked in the *Protagoras,* "Why may you not learn of him in the same way that you learned the arts of the grammarian or musician or trainer, not with the view of making any of them a profession, but only as a part of education and because a private gentleman ought to know them?"[3]

The Socratic Method

Socrates recognised the unscientific nature of the methods of the sophists, and his own method was essentially systematic and founded on general principles.[4] According to Aristotle, "There are two things which we may fairly attribute to Socrates, his inductive discourses and his universal definitions."[5] Inductive reasoning was his method of arriving at a definition. The result attained by his method could not be regarded as satisfying the requirements of scientific exactness, but this did not disturb Socrates, for he himself continually and emphatically disclaimed the possession of any knowledge, except perhaps the knowledge of his own limitations. The intoxicated Alcibiades says of him in the *Symposium*, "He knows nothing and is ignorant of all things — such is the appearance which he puts on."[6] Although not possessing knowledge himself, Socrates claimed to have the gift of discerning its presence in others, and of having the power to assist them to bring it to light.[7]

Task of Socrates

The first task of Socrates was to arouse men from that false self-satisfaction which was by him believed to be the cause of their misery, and to lead them to self-examination and self-criticism. He says, "Herein is the evil of ignorance, that he who is neither good nor wise is nevertheless satisfied with himself : he has no desire for that of which he feels no want."[8]

Socrates' mission was to make men feel this want to teach others what the utterance of the Delphic oracle had taught him — his own ignorance; to imbue them with a divine discontent; to make them feel, as Alcibiades puts it, 'the serpent's sting,' 'the pang of philosophy.'[9] In his defence Socrates neither disowned his mission nor his method : "I am that gadfly," he told his judges, "which God has attached to the state, and all day long and in all places am always fastening upon you, arousing and persuading and approaching you."[10]

Stages in Socratic Discourses

Three stages can generally be distinguished in the Socratic discourses : first, the stage called by Plato 'opinion,' in which the individual is unable to give valid reasons for his knowledge or supposed knowledge; second, the destructive or analytic stage, in which the individual is brought to realise that he does not know what he assumed he knows, and which leads to contradiction and a mental condition of doubt or perplexity; third, a synthetic stage for the results of which Plato would reserve the term 'knowledge.' When this last stage is attained, the individual's experience is critically reconstructed and he can justify his beliefs by giving the reasons for them.

Importance of Education to Plato

Education was a subject to which Plato attached the greatest importance. In The *Republic* he reckons it with war, the conduct of campaigns and the administration of states as amongst 'the grandest and most beautiful' subjects, and in *The Laws* he repeats that it is 'the first and fairest thing that the best of men can ever have.' In *The Laches*, which is professedly a treatise on education, he asks : 'Is this a slight thing about which you and Lysimachus are your riches; and upon their turning out well or ill depends the whole order of their father's house.' Again in *The Crito,*[11] he says : 'No man should bring children into the world who is unwilling to perse vere, to the end in their nurture and education.' The extent and elaborateness of the treatment of education in The *Republic* and in *The Laws* likewise testify to the importance of the subject in Plato's mind.

Difficulties in Sophist Education

The difficulties which arose from the educational methods of the sophists deeply perplexed Plato. His early dialogues everywhere bear the mark of this perplexity which, it seems, was common to the foremost minds of Greece at that time. The *Laches* records the concern of Lysimachus and Melesius as to the education of their children and their eagerness to accept guidance from any quarters, the Euthydemus ends with an appeal to Socrates by Crito concerning the education of Critobulus, his son.

Current Education in Greece

The type of education which was then current in Greece can be gathered from several references in the dialogues. In the *Crito* it is asked : "Were not the laws which have the charge of education right in commanding your father to train you in Music and Gymnastic?" The answer of Plato is : "Right, I should reply." In the *Protagoras* it is stated : "I am of opinion that skill in poetry was the principal part in education and this I conceive to be the power of knowing what compositions of the poets are correct, and what are not, and how they are to be distinguished and of explaining when asked the reason of the difference."[12] In *The Timaeus,* Critias says : "Now the day was that day of the Apaturia which is called the registration of youth, at which, according to custom, our parents gave prizes for recitations, and many of us sang the poems of Solon, which at that time had not gone out of fashion."[13]

Education of Greek Youth

The best account of the education of a Greek youth is the sketch given in *The Protagoras*. "Education and admonition commence in the first years of childhood, and last to the very end of life. Mother and nurse, and father and tutor are quarrelling about the improvement of the child as soon as ever he is able to understand them; he cannot say or do anything without setting forth to him that this is just and that is unjust; this is honourable, that is dishonourable; this is holy, that is unholy; do this and abstain from that. And if he obeys, well and good; if not, he is straightened by threats and blows, like a piece of warped wood. At a later stage they send him to teachers, and enjoin them to see to his manners even more than to his reading and music; and the teachers do as they are desired. And when the boy has learned his letters and is beginning to understand what is written, as before he understood only what was spoken, they put into his hands the works of great poets, which he reads at school; in these are contained many admonitions, and many tales and praises, and encomia of ancient famous men, which he is required to learn by heart, in order that he may imitate or emulate them and desire to become like them. Then, again, the teachers of the lyre take similar care that their young disciple is temperate and gets into no mischief; and when they taught him the use of the lyre, they introduce him to the poems of other excellent poets who are the lyric poets; and these they set to music, and make their harmonies and rhythms quite familiar to the children's souls, in order that they may learn to be more gentle and harmonious, and rhythmical, and so more fitted for speech and action; for the life of man in every part has need of harmony and rhythm. Then they send them to the master of gymnastic, in order that their bodies may better minister to the virtuous mind, and that they may not be compelled through bodily weakness to play the coward in war or any other occasion. This is what is done by those who have the means, and those who have the means are the rich; their children begin education soonest and leave off latest. When they have done with masters, the state again compels them to learn the laws, and live after the pattern which they furnish, and not after their own fancies; and just as in learning to write, the writing-master first draws lines with a style for the use of the young beginner, and gives him the tablet and makes him follow the lines, so the city draws the laws, which were the invention of good law-givers who were of old time; these are given to a young man, in order to guide him in his conduct whether as ruler or ruled; and he who transgresses them is to be corrected, or, in other words, called to account which is a term used not only in your country, but also in many others."[14]

Education of Greek Maiden

Xenophon's *The Economics* furnishes the complementary education of the Greek maiden. "Ah, Ischomachus, that is just what I (Socrates) should like particularly to learn from you. Did you yourself educate your wife to be all that a wife should be, or when you received her from her father and mother was she already a proficient well skilled to discharge the duties appropriate to a wife? Well skilled (he replied). What proficiency was she likely to bring with her, when she was not quite fifteen at the time she wedded me, and during the whole prior period of her life had been most carefully brought up to see and hear as little as possible, and to ask the fewest question? Or do you not think one should be satisfied, if at marriage her whole experience consisted in knowing how to take the wool and make a dress, and seeing how her mother's hand maidens had their daily spinning-tasks assigned them? For (he added) as regards control of appetite and self-indulgence (in reference to culinary matters), she had received the soundest education, and that I take to be the most important matter in the bringing up of man or woman."[15]

Plato's Own Theory of Education

Plato's own treatment of education is to be found in *The Republic*. Rousseau has said, "If you wish to know what is meant by public education, read Plato's *The Republic*. Those who merely judge books by their titles take this for a treatise on Politics, but it is the finest treatise on Education ever written."[16] Likewise Edward Caird has affirmed of *The Republic* that "perhaps it might best be described as a treatise on Education, regarded as the one great business of life from the beginning to the end of it."[17]

The Republic is professedly an inquiry into the nature of justice. But justice is essentially a social virtue. Aristotle said in Politics, "Justice has been acknowledged by us to be a social virtue." Consequently, to determine the nature of justice Plato is driven to construct in thought an ideal state wherein he hopes to find justice 'writ large.' Rousseau said in *Emile,* "It is true...that we have a very imperfect knowledge of the human heart if we do not also examine it in crowds; but it is none the less true that to judge of men we must study the individual man, and that he who had perfect knowledge of the inclinations of each individual might foresee all their combined effects in the body of the nation."[18]

Because of the multiplicity of human wants and of the insufficiency of any one individual to satisfy these by his own efforts, the state, in Plato's view, is necessary. It is likewise advantageous, since by reason of the diversity on the natural endowment of the individuals constituting the state the greatest efficiency can only be attained by the application of the principle of the division of labour and by cooperative effort. These two principles are implied in the oft-quoted statement of Aristotle :

"The state comes into existence originating in the bare needs of life."

The application of the principle of division of labour results in the separation of the citizens of the state into classes — the industrial or artisan and the guardian class, the duty of the former being to provide the necessaries of life, the duty of the latter being to enlarge the boundaries of the state — a proceeding which involves war — that luxuries may be available for the citizens and the state be something more than 'a community of swine.' The guardian class, Plato further subdivides into military and governing class, representing respectively the executive and deliberative functions of the government.

SCOPE OF EDUCATION

For each of the three classes of the community — the producing, the military and the governing — Plato ought to have provided, we should imagine, an appropriate form of training; but although the education of the soldier and that of the ruler or philosopher is treated at considerable length, no mention is made in *The Republic* of the education of the industrial class. The education of the members of this class, had Plato dealt with it, would doubtless have been of a strictly vocational nature, not, however, a state scheme of vocational training but something resembling rather 'the constitution of apprenticeship as it once existed in Modern Europe.' There would be no specific training in citizenship, for these members of the community have no voice in the government of the state; their characteristic virtue is obedience, technically 'temperance' — to know their place and to keep it.

The fact that this large element in the community is denied the benefits and privileges of citizenship, the communistic scheme has a serious defect in Plato's ideal state. It has been attributed to Plato's aristocratic prejudices, and to the Greek contempt for the mechanical arts. Artistotle regards the artisans as of even less account than the slaves, and maintains that they can only attain excellence as they become slaves, that is, come under the direction of a master. If, however, a state is to be safe, or be 'a unity' as Plato phrased it, all must share in the government. Contrasting the Greek with the modern ideal of virtue, T.H. Green says, "It is not the sense of duty to a neighbour, but the practical answer to the question who is my neighbour? that has varied." This explains the defect in Plato's scheme and helps us to appreciate the increased difficulty of our present day ethical, social and educational problems.

PRINCIPLES OF GUARDIAN'S EDUCATION

1. Improvement of the Soul. Plato's first treatment of education is the training of the guardians including the military and ruling classes. It is a general education governed mainly by the principle of imitation. Its two main divisions are the current forms of Greek education, namely, Music almost equivalent to the term Arts in a university curriculum and Gymnastic. But as Plato again warns us, "Neither are the two arts of Music and Gymnastic really designed, as is often supposed, the one for the training of the soul, the other for the training of the body. I believe that the teachers of both have in view chiefly the improvement of the soul."

2. Mental to precede Physical Education. At the outset of his treatment of education Plato asserts that "we should begin education with music and go on gymnastic afterwards; mental is thus to precede physical education. The care of the body ought to precede that of the soul, and the training of the appetite part should follow : none the less the case of it must be for the sake to the reason, and our care of the body for the sake of the soul."[19]

3. The Mother Tales. The mothers and nurses are to tell their children the authorised tales only : 'Let them fashion the mind with such tales, even more fondly they mould the body with their hands.'

Recognising the importance of first impressions Plato says, "The beginning is the most important part of any work, especially in the case of a young and tender thing."[20]

Consequently, consideration of the tales to be told to infants is not beneath the dignity of a philosopher.[21]

4. The Young should be trained in Both True and False. Music includes narratives and these are of two kinds, the true and the false. Somewhat paradoxically Plato maintains that the young should be trained in both, and that we should begin with the false fables. These are best suited to the child mind. He thus, recognises the truth of art as well as the truth of fact. But according to Plato not all fables should be taught, for a young person cannot judge what is allegorical and what is literal; anything that receives into his mind that age is likely to become indelible and unalterable; and therefore it is most important that the tales which the young first hear should be models of virtuous thoughts.[22]

5. Nothing must be admitted in Education Which does not conduce to the Promotion of Virtue. For 'true and false' Plato substitutes the standard 'good and evil.' He declines to take upon himself the task of composing fables suitable for children. But using as a criterion the principle just enunciated, he assumes a moral censorship over the tales then current. "The narrative of Hephaestus binding here his mother, and how on another occasion Zenus sent him flying for taking her part when she was being beaten, and all the battles of the gods in Homer — these tales must not be admitted into our state whether they are supposed to have an allegorical meaning or not."[23]

6. Stories about Gods. Plato proceeds to pass in review the stories about the gods and formulates the following theological canons :

(1) God is not the author of all things, but of good only — and the poet is not to be permitted to say that those who are punished are miserable and that God is the author of their misery.[24]

(2) The gods are not magicians who transform themselves, neither do they deceive mankind in any way. The tales to be told to children must conform to these principles, and others are not to be told to the children from their

youth upwards, if they are to honour the gods and their parents, and fables dealing with the gods, Plato proceeds to consider those relating to heroes and the souls of the departed. To make the citizens free men who should fear slavery more than death, the other world must not be reviled in fables but rather commended. All weeping and wailing of heroes must be expunged from fables : likewise all descriptions of violent laughter, for a fit of laughter which has been indulged to excess almost always produces a violent reaction.

7. High Value Set on Truth. In the tales to be recited to children in a high value is to be set upon truth; "if anyone at all is to have the privilege of lying, the rulers of the state should be the persons; and they, in their dealings either with their enemies or with their own citizens, may be allowed to lie for the public the kind." Temperance implying obedience to commanders and self-control in sensual pleasures is to be commended, while covetousness is to be condemned. The fables concerning heroes and others must accordingly be amended to agree with these principles.

The use is likewise to be forbidden of such language as implies that wicked men are often happy, and the good miserable; and that injustice is profitable when undetected, justice being a man's own loss and another's gain.

PRINCIPLES FORM OF NARRATIVES

Simple narration having thus discussed the matter of the narratives to be used in education, Plato addresses himself to a consideration of their forms.

1. No Imitation. In compositions he distinguishes between direct speech, which he calls 'imitation,' and indirect speech, which he calls 'simple narration.' 'Immitation' is only to be allowed of the speech and action of the virtuous man : the speeches of others are to be delivered and their actions described in the form of narration. The reason Plato gives is that imitation beginning in early youth and continuing far into life, as length grows into habits and becomes a second nature, affecting body, voice and mind.[25]

2. Discard of Effeminate and Convivial. In respect of music in its limited and modern sense, Plato maintains that all harmonies which are effeminate and convivial are to be discarded and only such retained as will make the citizens temperate and courageous. The rhythm is to be determined by the nature of the words, just as the style of words is determined by the moral disposition of the soul.

3. Art must be Moral. So must it be with the other arts and crafts, and not only the poets, but the professors of every other craft as well, must impress on their productions the image of the good.[26] Here we have the origin of the old quarrel between poetry and philosophy, or between art and morality. Plato will not entertain the idea of 'art for art's sake'; the only criterion he will recognise is the ethical.

4. Unconscious Assimilation. The reason of Plato's solicitude for a good and simple environment for the children who are to be the future guardians of the state is his belief in the efficacy of unconscious assimilation or imitation in the formation of character. As evidence of this we may cite the following, "We would not have our guardians grow up amid images of moral deformity, as in some noxious pasture, and there browse and feed upon many a baneful herb and flower, day by day, little by little, until they silently gather a festering mass of corruption in their own soul. Let our artists rather be those who are gifted to discern the true nature of the beautiful and graceful; then will our youth dwell in a land of health, amid fair sights and sounds, and receive the good in everything; and beauty, the effluence of fair works, shall flow into the eye and ear, like a health-giving breeze a purer region, and insensibly draw the soul from earliest years into likeness and sympathy with the beauty of reason."[27]

5. Rhythm and Harmony. "And therefore," Plato continues, "musical training is a more potent instrument than any other, because rhythm and harmony find their way into the inward places of soul, on which they mightily fasten, imparting grace, and making the soul of him who is rightly educated graceful, of him who is ill-educated ungraceful." That the result of a musical education should be the production of harmony and grace in the individual is repeated in the introduction to Plato's treatment of higher education or the education of the philosopher. There, he says, "music was the counterpart of gymnastic, and trained the guardians by the influences of habit, by harmony making them harmonious, by rhythm rhythmical."[28] The end throughout was the Greek ideal of manhood, a life which in itself was a work of art.

General Principles in Gymnastic

Plato's treatment of gymnastic in *The Republic* is decidedly brief;[29] he contents himself with indicating no more than the general principles. "Gymnastic as well as music should begin in early years; the training in it should be careful and should continue through life," he says, adding, however, "Now my belief is, not that good body by any bodily excellence improves the soul, but, on the contrary, that the good soul, by her own excellence, improves the body as far as this may be possible."

(i) *Moderate System* : Plato prescribes a simple moderate system such as would be productive of health and the utmost keenness of both eye and ear.[30] Of the habit of body cultivated by professional gymnasts he disapproves as unsuitable for men who have to undergo privations in war and variations in food when on a campaign. Abstinence from delicacies is also enjoined. The whole life, however, is not to be given up to gymnastics, for anyone who does nothing else ends by becoming uncivilised — "He is like a wild beast, all violence and fierceness, and knows no other way of dealing; and he lives in all ignorance and evil conditions, and has no sense of propriety and grace."[31]

Such then is, in outline, Plato's scheme of early training with its training in music and gymnastic. The dances which will be in vogue, the hunting and field exercises and the sports of the gymnasium and race-course, he adds,[32] must correspond with the foregoing outlines.

(ii) *No Training in Manual Arts* : There is one omission from this early education to which attention ought to be directed, for the omission is intentional on Plato's part; it is the absence of any reference to a training in the manual arts. The reason for the omission is incidentally disclosed by Plato in a later section of *The Republic*. All the useful arts were reckoned mean.[33]

(iii) *No Compulsion* : There are other omissions evidently un-intentional. The subjects of the higher education, Plato later rec-ognises, must begin in youth, hence in dealing with the education of the ruler or philosopher we find him stating : "Calculation and geometry and all the other elements of instruction, which are a preparation for dialectic, should be presented to the mind in childhood; not, however, under any notion of forcing our system of education."[34]

The principle of teaching-method here implied he elaborates by adding, "Bodily exercise, when compulsory, does no harm to the body; but knowledge which is acquired under compulsion, obtains no hold on the mind.... Then do not use compulsion, but let early education be a sort of amusement; you will then be better able to find out the natural bent." In *The Laws* the positive significance of play in education is emphasised. Thus, as has frequently been pointed out, we do not have to come to modern times, to Herbart, Froebel or Montessori, so find the child's interest or his play taken as a guiding principle in education : it is found formulated in Plato.

(iv) *Guidance to Guardians* : Those who are to undergo the early education and become guardians of the state are to unite in themselves "philosophy and spirit and swiftness and strength."[35] Throughout their education they are to be watched carefully and tested and tempted in various ways,[36] and those who, after being proved, come forth victorious and pure are to be appointed rulers and guardians of the state, the others remaining auxiliaries or soldiers.

HIGHER EDUCATION

Principles of Qualifications

The qualities required for the higher education, or for the philosophic character Plato frequently enumerates. Preference is to be given to "the surest and the bravest, and, if possible, to the fairest and, having noble and generous tempers, they should also have the natural gifts which will facilitate their education."[37] Another account runs, "A good memory and quick to learn, noble, gracious, the friend of truth, justice, courage, temperance,"[38] again, "Courage, magnificence, apprehension, memory."[39]

Aims and Objectives

The aim of the higher education is not a mere extension of knowledge; it is, in Plato's phrase, "the conversion of a soul from study of the sensible world to contemplation of real existence."[40] "Then, if I am right," he explains, "certain professors of education must be wrong when they say that they can put a knowledge into the soul which was not there before, like sight into blind eyes. Whereas our argument shows that the power and capacity of learning exist in the soul already; and that jus as the eye was unable to turn from darkness to light without the whole body, so too the instrument of knowledge can only by the movement of the whole soul be turned from the world of becoming into that of being, and learn by degrees to endure the sight of being, and of the brightest and best of being, or in other words, of the good."[41]

Scope and Scheme

Such is the aim of the higher education, the education of the philosopher or ruler. Plato, having determined the aim, next proceeds to consider the scope of higher education. It includes number or arithmetic, plane and solid geometry, astronomy, theory of music or harmonics, all dialectic. Through Mathematics to Metaphysics might be said to sum up Plato's scheme of higher education.

Principles deciding the Selection of the Higher Studies

The higher education must lead to reflection rather than deal with the things of sense;[42] they must likewise be of universal application.[43] The first subject that satisfies these requirements is number, hence Plato concludes, "This is a kind of knowledge which legislation may fitly prescribe; and we must endeavour to persuade those who are to be the principal men of our state to go and learn arithmetic, not as amateurs, but they must carry on the study until they see the nature of numbers with the mind only; nor again, like merchants or retail-traders, with a view to buying or selling, but for the sake of their military use, and of the soul herself; and because this will be the easiest way for her to pass from becoming to truth and being."[44] The main function of number is thus to afford a training in abstraction.

Search for Universal Notions

The value which Plato assigns to number, as a subject in the training preparatory to philosophy, strikes the modern mind as somewhat exaggerated. This can be explained, however, by the fact that philosophers had then only begun the search for universal or conceptual notions, and the science of number presented itself as satisfying their requirements in a remarkable degree. The Pythagoreans had indeed maintained that number was the rational principle or essence of things, and it is generally agreed that Plato was for sometime under Pythagorean influence; in fact, by some it is maintained that by 'Ideas' he understood, at one stage in the development of that doctrine, nothing other than numbers themselves. At the time of writing *The Republic*, however, he had outgrown the naïve identification of numbers with things themselves, for we find him asserting, "Yet anybody who has the least acquaintance with geometry will not deny that such a conception of the science is in flat contradiction to the ordinary language of geometricians. They have in view practice only, and are always speaking, in a narrow and ridiculous manner, of squaring and extending and applying and the like — they confuse the necessities of geometry with those of daily life; whereas knowledge is the real object of the whole science."[45] If the Greeks, as is implied in Plato's statement, were at times in danger in ignoring the purely conceptual nature of number, we of the present day are in danger of disregarding the practical needs which brought the science into existence and the concrete bases in which numbers were first exemplified.

Principle of Transfer of Training

In insisting on the value of number as a means of training in abstraction, Plato gives expression to a statement which implies the doctrine of formal discipline or transfer of training, that is, that a training in one function results in a general improvement of the mind, which in turn favourably influences other functions. Thus he asks, "Have you further observed, that those who have a natural talent for calculation are generally quick at every other kind of knowledge; and even the dull if they have had an arithmetical training, although they may derive no other advantage from it, always become much quicker than they would otherwise have been?"[46] When in the same section he adds, "And indeed, you will not easily find a more difficult subject, and not many as difficult," he approximates to the doctrine that the more trouble a subject causes the better training it affords, the fallacy of philosopher, namely, it matters not what you teach a pupil provided he does not want to learn it. This argument is repeated in almost identical terms in *The Laws*. "Arithmetic stirs up him who is by nature sleepy and dull, and makes him quick to learn, retentive, shrewd, and aided by art divine he makes progress quite beyond his natural powers."[47]

In dealing with geometry Plato also remarks that "In all departments of knowledge, as experience proves, any one who has studied geometry is infinitely quicker of apprehension than one who has not."[48]

Mathematics and Dialectic

These views must nevertheless be qualified by the statement occurring in the discussion of the relation between mathematics and dialectic. "For you surely would not regard the skilled mathematician as a dialectician? Assuredly not, he said : I have hardly ever known a mathematician who was capable of reasoning."[49] This qualification, it has been contended,[50] acquits Plato of the responsibility of initiating the doctrine of formal training, but if it does so, it is only at the cost of consistency. In his defence, however, it may be said, that in Plato's days little was known of, although much was hoped from the science of number; and no objection could have been urged against him had he said that a knowledge of number 'broadened' rather than 'quickened' the mind. Number, like language, affords us an invaluable means of mastering and controlling experience, and does not require to be defended on the ground of some hypothetical influence on the mind in general. It must be put to Plato's credit that in interpreting a faculty as a function he avoided the 'faculty' doctrine which long retarded the development of psychology.[51]

Geometry : Vision of the Idea of Good

As Number is the first subject selected for inclusion in the curriculum of the higher education, so geometry is the second. Its bearing on strategy is acknowledged, but what Plato is concerned about is whether it tends in any degree to make easier the vision of the idea of good.[52] The idea of good, or 'the Form of the Good,' is the ultimate principle in Plato's philosophy, at once the source of all Being and of all knowledge. This, he believes, geometry does accomplish; "geometry will draw the soul towards truth, and create the spirit of philosophy,"[53] consequently those who are to be the rulers of the ideal state must be directed to apply themselves to the study of geometry.

The study of solid geometry, or the investigation of space of three dimensions, should, Plato admits, logically follow plane geometry and in turn precede astronomy, or the study of solid bodies in motion, but the unsatisfactory condition of the subject at the time causes him to dismiss it briefly.

Astronomy : Re-illumination of Eye of the Soul

Astronomy is the next of the instrumental subjects of the higher training, and in enumerating its practical advantages to the agriculturist and navigator Plato remarks, "I am amused at your fear of the world, which makes you guard against the appearance of insisting upon useless studies; and I quite admit the difficulty of believing that in every man there is an eye of the soul, which, when by other pursuits lost and dimmed, is by these purified and re-illumined; and is more precious than ten thousand bodily eyes, for by it alone is truth seen."[54] "Then in astronomy, as in geometry, we should employ problems, and let the heavens alone if we would approach the subject in the right way and so make the natural gift of reason to be of any real use."[55] In accordance with this principle the calculation of Neptune into existence by Adams and Leverrier would have been commended by Plato; the verification of its existence by actual observation would have merited his contempt.

Theory of Music

The last of the studies preparatory to dialectic is music, not, however, music as an art as dealt with in the early education, but the theory of music, harmonics, the mathematical relations existing between notes, chords, etc., or what we should now probably term the physical bases of music, "a thing," Plato affirms, "which I would call useful; that is, if sought after with a view to the beautiful and good; but if pursued in any other spirit, useless."[56]

If a common basis for the mathematical studies just enumerated could be discovered, Plato believes that it would advance the end in view, namely, preparation for the science of dialectic.

Dialectic : Revelation of Absolute Truth

Dialectic is, for Plato, the highest study of all. It is as far removed from the mathematical sciences as they are from the practical arts. The sciences assume certain hypotheses, or make certain assumptions; geometry for example, assumes the existence of space and does not inquire whether it is a perceptual datum, a conceptual construction or, as Kant maintained, an a priori *Welt Anschauung*. Philosophy or dialectic as Plato calls it, tries to proceed without presuppositions or, at least, seeks critically to examine their validity and to determine the extent of their application.

"I must remind you," says Plato, "that the power of dialectic can also reveal this (absolute truth), and only to one who is a disciple of the previous sciences." "And assuredly," he continues "no one will argue that there is any other method of comprehending by any regular process all true existence of ascertaining what each thing is in its own nature; for the arts in general are concerned with the desires and opinions of men, or are cultivated with a view to production and construction, or for the preservation of such productions and constructions; and as to the mathematical sciences which, as we were saying, have some apprehension of true being — geometry and the like — they only dream about being, but never can they behold the waking reality too long as they leave the hypotheses which they use unexamined, and are unable to give an account of them. For when a man knows not his own first principle, and when the conclusion and intermediate steps are also constructed out of he knows not what, how can be imagine that such fabric of convention can ever become science?"[57] In *The Cratylus* Plato defined the dialectician as "he who knows how to ask questions and how to answer them." In *The Phaedrus* he identifies dialectic with the process of division and generalisation, and he adds, "For according as a man can survey a subject as a whole or not, he is or is not a dialectician."[58]

"The dialectic, and dialectic alone, goes directly to the first principle and is the only science which does away with hypotheses in order to make her ground secure; the eye of the soul, which is literally buried in an outlandish slough, is by her gentle aid lifted upwards; and she uses as handmaids and helpers in the work of conversion, the sciences which we have been discussing."

Dialectic then is the coping-stone of the sciences.[59] No other science can be placed higher; it completes the series. All who would be magistrates in the ideal state must consequently address themselves to such studies as will enable them to use the weapons of the dialectician most scientifically.

No Intellectual Study for Cadets

Having determined the subjects which the philosopher or ruler must study, Plato proceeds to consider the distributions of these studies.[60] For three years after the completion of the early education, that is, from seventeen to twenty years of age, the youths are to serve as cadets, being brought into field of the battle, and, "like young hounds, have a taste of blood given them."

During these years of bodily exercises there is to be no intellectual study, "for sleep and exercise are unpropitious to learning."

No Serious Study in Youth

At the age of twenty the choiced cadets are to be selected to undergo the mathematical training preparatory to dialectic. This training is to continue for ten years, and at the age of thirty a further selection is to be made, and those who are chosen are to begin the study of dialectic.[61] Plato deliberately withholds the study of dialectic to this late age, giving as his reason that "youngsters, when they first get the taste in their mouths, argue for amusement, and are always contradicting and refuting others in imitation of those who refute them; like puppy-dogs, they rejoice in pulling and tearing at all who come near them."[62] According to Aristotle, "The young man is not a fit student of politics."[63] This study is to be prosecuted for five years, every other pursuit being resigned for it. For the next fifteen years, that is, from thirty-five to fifty years of age, the philosophers or rulers are to return to practical life, take the command in war and hold such offices of state as befit 'young men.'

After the age of fifty, the lives of the rulers are to be spent in contemplation of 'the Good,' so that when they are called upon to regulate the affairs of the state, their knowledge of this will serve as a pattern according to which they are to order the state and the lives of individuals, and the remainder of their own lives also; "making philosophy their chief pursuit, but when their turn comes, toiling also at politics and ruling for the public good, not as though they were performing some heroic action, but simply as a matter of duty; and when they have brought up in each generation others like themselves, they will depart to the Islands of the Blest and dwell there."[64]

WOMEN'S EDUCATION

Such is Plato's scheme of education as set forth in *The Republic*, and he warns us in conclusion that it is an education for women as well as for men; they are to have the same training and education, a training in music and gymnastic, and in the art of war, which they must practise like men, "for you must not suppose," he adds, "that what I have been saying applies to men only and not to women as far as their natures can go."[65]

Plato dismisses as irrelevant the ridicule which would be excited by his proposal that women should share with men the exercises of the gymnasia, maintaining that the question should be decided on principle. The principle, he argues, which applies in this case is that each member of the state should undertake the work for which he is the best fitted by nature, and while admitting that physically the woman is weaker than the man, he nevertheless maintains that in respect to political or governing ability the woman is the equal of the man. Had he affirmed that in respect of intellectual ability the woman is on the average the equal of the man, he would have anticipated the conclusions of modern research.

Co-education Proposal

Plato's co-educational proposal arouses distrust, not so much on its own account but because the second 'wave,' the community of wives and children, results from fit.[66] The great wave or paradoxes in the construction of Plato's ideal state are : (1) the community of goods and of pursuits; (2) the community of wives and children; (3) summarised in the statement — "Until kings are philosophers or philosophers are kings, cities will never cease from ill." To secure the end to preserve the unity of the state, Plato was forced to destroy the family as the social unit. The family with its bonds of kinship and ties of natural affection was the only institution which he feared might challenge the supremacy, or lead to the disruption, of the state, and the pains he displays to eliminate every trace of family influences are witness of its power. Plato could only secure the unity of the state at the cost of sacrificing all differences; he makes a wilderness and calls it peace. This is the great defect of his ideal state, and on this ground his communistic scheme has been effectively criticised by Aristotle.[67] A similar criticism has been applied by Rousseau, who says, "I am quite aware that Plato, in *The Republic*, assigns the same gymnastics to women and men. Having got rid of the family, there is no place for women in his system of government, so he is forced to turn them into men. That great genius has worked out his plans in detail and has provided against a difficulty which in all likelihood no one would ever have raised; but he has not succeeded in meeting the real difficulty. I am not speaking of the alleged community of wives which has often been laid to his charge; ...I refer to that sub-version of all the tenderest of our natural feelings, which he sacrificed to an artificial sentiment which can only exist for their aid. Will the bonds of convention hold firm without some foundation in nature? Can devotion to the state exist apart from the love of those near and dear to us? Can patriotism thrive except in the soil of that miniature fatherland, the home? Is it not the good son, the good husband, the good father, who makes the good citizen?"

EDUCATION IN LAWS

In *The Laws*, the work of his old age, Plato readdresses himself to the subject of education. The dialogue commencing with a consideration of the laws of Minos drifts into a consideration of the perfect citizen ruler and how to train him — into a discussion on education, in short. Disillusioned by the experiences of life, Plato in *The Laws*, so some interpreters maintain, recants the idealistic schemes which he projected in

The Republic; in the latter work he does not, however, really abandon his earlier principles, but rather seeks to illustrate their application in practice. He describes, if not the ideal city, the pattern of which is laid up in heaven, at least "the second best," which might be realisable "in present circumstances."[68]

Similar Aim of Education

The treatment of education in *The Laws* supplements that in *The Republic*, emphasising the practical aspects and thus approximating to Artistotle's treatment of education in the *Politics*. The aim of education nevertheless remains the same, for as Plato says in *The Laws*, "At present when we speak in terms of praise or blame about the bringing up of each person, we call one man educated and another uneducated, although the uneducated man may be sometimes very well educated for the calling of a retail trader, or of a captain of a ship, and the like. For we are not speaking of education in this narrower sense, but of that other education in virtue from youth upwards, which makes a eagerly pursue the ideal perfection of citizenship, and teaches him how rightly to rule and how to obey. This is the only education which, upon our view, deserves the name; that other sort of training, which aims at the acquisition of wealth or bodily strength, or mere cleverness apart from intelligence and justice, is mean and illiberal, and is not worthy to be called education at all. But let us not quarrel with one another about a word, provided that the preposition which has just been granted holds good; to wit, that those who are rightly educated generally become good men. Neither must we cast a slight upon education, which is the first and fairest thing that the best of men can ever have, and which, though liable to take a wrong direction, is capable of reformation, and this business of reformation is the greatest business of every man while he lives."[69]

Universal Education

Education in *The Laws* is to be universal, not restricted as in *The Republic* to the guardian class, and is to be compulsory, "the children shall come (to the schools) not only if their parents please, but if they do not please; there shall be compulsory education, as the saying is, of all and sundry, as far as this is possible; and the pupils shall be regarded as belonging to the state rather than to their parents. My law shall apply to females as well as males; they shall both go through the same exercises."[70] To the co-educational principles and the communistic scheme on which it is based Plato frequently alludes in *The Laws*, thus indicating that the proposal in *The Republic* was regarded by him as a serious one. In support of the idea that women and girls should undergo the same gymnastic and military exercises as men and boys, Plato states, "While they are yet girls they should have practised dancing in arms and the whole art of fighting — when grown up women, they should apply themselves to evolutions and tactics, and the mode of grounding and taking up arms; if for no other reason, yet in case the whole military force should have to leave the city and carry on operations of war outside, that those who will have to guard the young and the rest of the city may be equal to the task; and, on the other hand, when enemies, whether barbarian or Hellenic, come from without mighty force and make a violent assault upon them, and thus compel them to fight for the possession of the city, which is far from being an impossibility, great would be the disgrace to the state, if the women had been so miserably trained they would not fight for their young, as birds will, against any creative however strong, or die or undergo any danger, but must instantly rush to the temples and crowd at the altars and shrines, and bring upon human nature the reproach, that of all animals man is the most cowardly."[71]

The Curriculum

The main subjects in the curriculum proposed in *The Laws* are the same as those given in *The Republic* — for the early education music and gymnastic, and for the higher education mathematics, dialectic, the study to which the mathematical subjects were merely preparatory in *The Republic*, is alluded to only indirectly in the more practical *The Laws*.

(1) Gymnastic. Gynastic occupies a more prominent place

than it does in *The Republic*, where it was treated merely in outline. It is now divided into two branches, dancing and wrestling, and these are, in turn, further, subdivided. "One sort of dancing imitates musical recitation, and aims at preserving dignity and freedom; the other aims at producing health, agility and beauty in the limbs and parts of the body, giving the proper flexion being diffused everywhere, and forming a suitable accompaniment to the dance."[72] In regard to wrestling, that form "of wrestling erect and keeping free the neck and hands and sides, working with energy and constancy, with a composed strength, and for the sake of health is useful and is to be enjoined alike on masters and scholars."[73] The general aim is that of all movements wrestling is most akin to the military art, and is to be pursued for the sake of this, and not for the sake of wrestling.[74]

(2) Music. Plato's treatment of music in *The Laws* follows the lines of that in *The Republic*, the old quarrel between poetry and philosophy being frequently renewed.[75] The same conclusion is reached, namely, that the compositions must impress on the minds of the young the principle "that the life which is by the Gods deemed to be the happiest is also the best."[76]

(3) Craft. The omission in *The Republic* of any reference to the education of the industrial or artisan class is partially rectified in *The Laws*. "According to my view," Plato now says, "anyone who would be good at anything must practise that thing from his youth upwards, both in sport and earnest, in its several branches : for example, he who is to be a good builder, should play at building children's houses; he who is to be a good husband man, at tilling the ground; and those who have the care of their education should provide them when young with mimic tools. They should learn beforehand the knowledge which they will afterwards require for their art. For example, the future carpenter should learn to measure or apply the line in play; and the future warrior should learn riding, or some other exercise, for amusement, and the teacher should endeavour to direct the children's inclinations and pleasures, by the help of amusements, to their final aim in life. The most important part of education is right training in the nursery. The soul of the child in his play should be guided by the love of that sort of excellence in which when he grows up to manhood he will have to be perfected."[77]

Early Training

As in *The Republic* so in *The Laws*, education cannot begin too early, "Am I not right in maintaining that a good education is that which tends most to the improvement of mind and body? And nothing can be plainer than that the fairest bodies are those which grow up from infancy in the best and straightest manner."[78] The care of the child even before birth is dealt with by Plato.[79] The early discipline is to be, as with Aristotle, habituation to the good and the beautiful. "Now I mean by education that training which is given by suitable habits to the first instincts of virtue in children; when pleasure, and friendship, and pain, and hatred are rightly implanted in souls not yet capable of understanding the nature of them, and who find them, after they have obtained reason, to be in harmony with her. This harmony of the soul, taken as a whole, is virtue; but the particular training in respect to pleasure and pain, which leads you always to hate what you ought to hate, and love what you ought to love from the beginning of life to the end, may be separated off; and, in my view, will be rightly called education."[80]

The early training in *The Republic* comprising music and gymnastic was designed to occupy the first seventeen years of life. The ages at which the various parts of these subjects were to be taken up were not further particularised. In *The Laws*, however, Plato is most precise as to the occupations of the early years and the time to be allotted to each. "Up to the age of three years, whether of boy or girl, if a person strictly carries out previous regulations and makes them a principal aim, he will do much for the advantage of the young creatures. But at three, four, five or even six years the childish nature will require sport.... Children at that age have certain natural modes of amusement which they find out for themselves when they meet."[81]

(4) Sports. The sports which the children at these early ages engage in, it may be interpolated, are, in Plato's opinion, of supreme significance in maintaining the stability of the state. In *The Republic*[82] Plato repeatedly expresses his fear of innovations in music and gymnastic lest these should imperil the whole order of society. This was natural, for any change in an ideal state could only be regarded as a change for the worse. It was also in accordance with the Greek attitude of mind, to which the modern ideal of an infinite progress brought about by constant innovations was abhorrent, and which conceived of perfection after the manner of the plastic arts as limited and permanent. In *The Laws*, even when the constitution is but 'second best,' the dread of innovations still haunts Plato, and leads him to observe "that the plays of children have a great deal to do with the permanence or want of permanence in legislation. For when plays are ordered with a view to children having the same plays, and amusing themselves after the same manner, and finding delight in the same playthings, the more solemn institutions of the state are allowed to remain undisturbed. Whereas if sports are disturbed, and innovations are made in them, and they constantly change, and the young never speak of their having the same likings, or the same established notions of good and bad taste, either in the bearing of their bodies or in their dress, but he who devises something new and out of the way in figures and colours and the like is held in special honour, we may say that no greater evil can happen in the state; for he who changes these sports is secretly changing the manners of the young, and making the old to be dishonoured among them and the new to be honoured. And I affirm that there is nothing which is a greater injury to all states than saying this."[83]

Up to the age of six the children of both sexes may play together. After the age of six, however, they were to be separated. "Let boys live with boys, and girls in like manner with girls. Now they must begin to learn — the boys going to the teachers of horsemanship and the use of the bow, the javelin and sling, and the girls too, if they do not object, at any rate until they know how to manage these weapons, and especially how to handle heavy arms."[84]

The musical is to alternate with the gymnastic training. "A fair time for a boy of ten years old to spend in letters is three years; the age of thirteen is the proper time for him to begin to handle the lyre, and he may continue at this for another three years, neither more nor less, and whether his father or himself like or dislike the study, he is not to be allowed to spend more or less time in learning music than the law allows."[85]

Studies Suitable for Freemen

There still remain three studies suitable for freemen. Arithmetic is one of them; the measurement of length, surface and depth is the second; and the third has to do with the revolutions of the stars in relation to one another. Not everyone has need to toil through all these things in a strictly scientific manner, but only a few.[86] All that is required for the many is such a knowledge as "every child in Egypt is taught when he learns the alphabet, and which frees them from that natural ignorance of all these things which is so ludicrous and disgraceful."[87] He who is to be a good ruler of the state, must, however, make a complete study of these subjects and of their interconnections; he must know these two principles — "that the soul is the oldest of all things which are born, and is immortal and rules over all bodies; moreover, he who has not contemplated the mind of nature which is said to exist in the stars, and gone through the previous training, and seen the connection of music with these things."

Director of Education

While in *The Republic* education was to be in the immediate charge of the guardians of the state, in *The Laws* it is to be delegated to a Director of Education.[88] The end of education nevertheless remains the same. Education is for the good of the individual and for the safety of the state. Thus Plato reaffirms in *The Laws*, "If you ask what is the good of education in general, the answer is easy — that education makes good men, and that good men act nobly, and conquer their enemies in battle, became they are good. Education certainly gives victory, although victory sometimes produces forgetfulness of education, for many have grown insolent from victory in war, and this insolence has engendered in them innumerable evils; and many a victory has been and will be suicidal to the victors; but education is never suicidal."[89]

LIMITATION OF PLATO'S PRINCIPLES

Plato established the humanistic tradition in Western education. His influence on later educational thought can be treated in quintillion, in the mediaeval curriculum, the studies constituting the trivium (grammar, rhetoric, logic or dialectic) and the quadrivium (music, arithmetic, geometry, astronomy), if different in order, being practically identical with those prescribed by Plato for the philosophers, in More's *Utopia*, Elyot's *Governor* and other renaissance writers, in the educational scheme of the *Book of Discipline* ascribed to John Knov, in Rousseau's *Article on Political Economy* and in Fichte's *Addresses to the German Nation*. Whether this influence has been for good or evil has been vigorously debated. That different interpretations can be derived from the writings of a thinker so original and fertile as Plato is only to be expected.

1. *Static View of State* : Thus, Plato's static view of the state, with divisions into clearly demarcated classes, each of which is required to keep as much as possible to itself, has been condemned as undemocratic.

2. *Neglect of Technical Education* : Another evil side of Platonic system, according to Whitehead, was its total neglect of technical education as an ingredient in the complete development of ideal human beings. On the other hand, Whitehead recognises that the Platonic ideal has rendered imperishable service to European civilisation by encouraging art, by fostering that spirit of disinterested curiosity which is the origin of science and by maintaining the dignity of mind in the face of material force. Dewey likewise acclaims Plato's procedure of untrammelled

inquiry, remarking, "Nothing could be more helpful to present philosophising than a 'Back to Plato' movement; but it would have to be back to the dramatic, restless, co-operatively inquiring Plato of the Dialogues, trying one mode of attack after another to see what it might yield; back to Plato whose highest flight of metaphysics always terminated with a social and practical turn, and not to the artificial Plato constructed by unimaginative commentators who treat him as the original university professor."[90]

EVALUATION

As has been pointed out earlier, Rousseau was correct when he commented that Plato's *The Republic* is the finest textbook on education. But it must be admitted that Plato's scheme of education suffers from certain defects and shortcomings, which have been enumerated below :

1. *Little Education to the Productive Class* : In any society the labouring or productive class is invariably the largest in size. In Plato's scheme of education, this class is granted only primary education, which implies that higher education of all kinds is intended only for the soldiers and the governing classes, assuming that the labouring class has no need for such an education. Plato's dictum was that the productive class actually required no more than primary education.

2. *Absence of Variety* : Plato's educational plan pays no attention to the individual differences between one individual and another. He suggested the same kind of education to be given to an entire class of people, according to a uniform curriculum. This will inevitably lead to the creation of only one kind of citizens, thus inevitably leading to deadening monotony and lack of variety, which kills all future progress.

3. *Stress on Philosophy* : Some people have got the impression that Plato's insistence on philosophy is exaggerated, and that it could only lead to an increase in the number of contemplative individuals at the expense of more practical numbers. But it must be remembered that Plato has stressed the

importance of both bodily and mental development and in this respect, he has achieved a remarkable harmony of both.

4. *Neglect of Literary Education* : Plato's curriculum also neglects training in literature by stressing the importance of training in mathematics.

In spite of the above defects, Plato's concept of education has influenced educational philosophy in almost all ages. In particular, his influence can be seen in the idealist philosophy of education. And, many of the finest teachers still consider Plato as their only true guide.

REFERENCES

1. *Laches*, 186.
2. *Meno*, 92.
3. *Protagoras,* 312.
4. Livingstone, R.W., *Potrait of Socrates* (Oxford University Press, 1938).
5. Aristotle, *Metaphysics*, 1078.
6. *Symposium*, 216.
7. Cf. metaphor of midwife in *Theaetetus*, 150; also *Symposium*, 209.
8. *Symposium*, 204.
9. *Ibid.*, 217.
10. *Apology*, 31.
11. *Crito,* 50.
12. *Protagoras*, 339.
13. *Timaeus*, 21.
14. *Protagoras*
15. *The Works of Xenophon*, translated by H.G. Dakyns (London : Macmillan & Co., Ltd., 1897), Vol. III, Part I, pp. 226-27.
16. *Emile,* Everyman's translation, p. 8.
17. Edward, C., *Evolution of Theology in the Greek Philosophers* (Glasgow : J. Maclehose & Sons, 1904), p. 140.
18. *Emile*, p. 202.
19. *The Republic,* 377.
20. Cf. Aristotle, *Politics*, vii, 17.
21. *The Republic*, 376.
22. *Ibid.*, 378.
23. *Ibid.*, 378.
24. *Ibid.*, 380.

25. *Ibid.*, 395.
26. *Ibid.*, 401.
27. *Ibid.*, 401.
28. *Ibid.*, 522.
29. *Ibid.*, 403-12.
30. *The Republic*, 404.
31. *Ibid.*, 411.
32. *Ibid.*, 412.
33. *Ibid.*, 522.
34. *Ibid.*, 536.
35. *Ibid.*, 376.
36. *Ibid.*, 413.
37. *The Republic*, 535.
38. *Ibid.*, 487.
39. *Ibid.*, 490.
40. *Ibid.*, 521.
41. *Ibid.*, 518.
42. *Ibid.*, 523.
43. *Ibid.*, 522.
44. *Ibid.*, 525.
45. *Ibid.*, 527.
46. *The Republic*, 526.
47. *The Laws*, 747.
48. *The Republic*, 752.
49. *Ibid*, 531.
50. Moore, E.C., *What is Education?* (Boston and London : Ginn & Co, 1915), Ch. iii.
51. *The Republic*, 477.
52. *Ibid.*, 527.
53. *Ibid.*, 528.
54. *The Republic*, 537.
55. *Ibid.*, 530.
56. *Ibid.*, 531.
57. *Ibid.*, 533.
58. *Ibid.*, 537.
59. *Ibid.*, 334.
60. *Ibid.*, 537-41.
61. *Ibid.*, 536.
62. *Ibid.*, 539.

63. Aristotle, *Ethics.*
64. *The Republic*, 540.
65. *Ibid.*
66. *The Republic*, 457.
67. Aristotle, *Politics*, ii, 3.
68. *The Laws*, 739, 753.
69. *Ibid.*, 643-44.
70. *Ibid.*, 804.
71. *Ibid.*, 814.
72. *Ibid.*, 795.
73. *Ibid.*, 796.
74. *Ibid.*, 814.
75. *Ibid.*, 659-70.
76. *Ibid.*, 664.
77. *Ibid.*, 643.
78. *Ibid.*, 788.
79. *Ibid.*, 788-92.
80. *Ibid.*, 653.
81. *Ibid.*, 794.
82. *Ibid.*, 424.
83. *The Laws*, 794.
84. *Ibid.*
85. *Ibid.*, 810.
86. *Ibid.*, 817-18.
87. *Ibid.*, 819.
88. *The Laws*, 765-66.
89. *Ibid.*, 641.
90. *Contemporary American Philosophy* (London : George Allen & Unwin Ltd., 1930), II, p. 21.

2

ARISTOTLE

(384-322 B.C.)

According to Frank Thilly, "In its scope, Aristotle's philosophy is perhaps the most comprehensive synthesis of knowledge ever achieved by the mind of man. No other thinker, ancient, medieval, or modern — with the possible exception of the German philosopher Hegel — has incorporated into his system so great a bulk of knowledge."[1] Among the pioneers of human knowledge, Aristotle was undoubtedly the greatest. His philosophy included almost all the sciences and humanities such as logic, ethics, mathematics, physics, biology and psychology, metaphysics and political science. He was not merely an eclectic. Far from it, he was the original genius behind the original growth of not only so many social sciences but also the physical science. His influence in philosophy surpassed even that of his master Plato. It could be seen not only on the philosophy propounded by the thinkers of the Middle Ages but also upon the philosophical systems of the modern western philosophy such as that of Spinoza, Immanuel Kant and Hegel. His position in the history of philosophy is unique. From the criteria of breadth, originality and influence, Aristotle was undoubtedly, "Master of those who know."

BIOGRAPHICAL SKETCH

Born in 384 B.C., in Stagira, a city of Greece, Aristotle had a silver spoon in his mouth right from his childhood. His father, Nicomachus, was the court physician of Philip of Macedon.[2]

Aristotle entered the famous Academy of the great philosopher Plato at the early age of seventeen years. He stayed there for almost twenty years as a student and a teacher. In 347 B.C. after the death of his master Plato, Aristotle left the Academy and started travelling. He went to Assos in Mysia and from there to Mitylene. He was called by the king Philip to look after the education of his son Alexander the Great, in 342 B.C. For seven years he was the tutor of Alexander after which he returned to Athens to establish the school known as Lyceum. It was also known as Peripatetic school because of the habit of Aristotle of walking while lecturing. His method of teaching was not only through lectures but also through dialogues. After the death of Alexander the Great he was accused of sacrilege. He left Athens for Euboea where he died in 322 B.C.

Aristotle was a master of dialectic. He was a great observer, a voracious reader and a specialist in both the natural sciences as well as in philosophy. Among his writings one finds not only on metaphysics and logic but also on human sciences like psychology and ethics and politics as well as upon natural sciences.

WORKS OF ARISTOTLE

It has been said that Aristotle wrote as many as 400 books.[3] Each book, however, means a chapter of a book as we generally understand by the term 'book' today.

Aristotle's works have been classified into those of logic, metaphysics, ethics, politics, rhetoric, psychology and natural sciences. In these fields his important works are as follows :

1. Logic. Aristotle's views concerning logic are available in his work *Organen*. This work includes categories, rules of interpretations, analytic and fallacies, etc. This great work is divided into different books on these different topics.

2. Metaphysics. *On metaphysics* includes as many as 14 books of Aristotle.

3. Ethics. Aristotle's famous work *Nicomachean Ethics*

consists of 10 books on different topics concerning ethics. Another important work on ethics is Eudemian ethics.

4. Politics. Aristotle's famous book *Politics* consists of eight books. Besides this important work he also wrote another book entitled *On the Constitution of Athens*. It contains Aristotle's philosophy of education as well.

5. Psychology. Aristotle's famous work *On the Soul* consists of eight books on different topics concerning human psychology. Besides, he also wrote small independent treaties on memory, dream, etc.

6. Natural Sciences. Aristotle had a wide influence on almost all the natural sciences due to his pioneering work in different fields. Of these the most important were : *Physics* (eight books of which Book VII is an interpolation); *Astronomy* (four books); *Origin and Decay* (two books); *Meteorology* (four books); *Cosmology* (spurious); *Botany* (spurious); *History of Animals* (ten books); *On the parts of Animals* (four books); *On the Progression of Animals* (not genuine, according to some); *On the Origin of Animals* (five books); *On the Lecomotion of Animals* (spurious).

From the point of view of the period of writing, Aristotle's works are classified into the following three periods :

1. Writings of Platonic Age. These were written during Aristotle's stay in Plato's Academy. Of these the most important is — *On the End.*

2. Writings in the Court of Macedon. While the first class of writings has a influence of Plato, the writings during this period were more free and original. Of these the most important are — Aristotle's work on Metaphysics and Politics.

3. Writings in Lyceum. These writings were composed in Aristotle's school known as Lyceum. Of these the most important are — *On Creation and Destruction* and *On Heavens*, etc.

Ethics and Politics

The Politics of Aristotle is the second part of a treatise of which the Ethics is the first part. It looks back to the Ethics as the Ethics looks forward to the Politics. Aristotle did not separate the spheres of the statesman and the moralist. In the Ethics he has described the character necessary for the good life, but that life is for him essentially to be lived in society. In the last chapters of the Ethics he comes to the practical application of his inquiries, that finds expression not in moral exhortations addressed to the individual but in a description of the legislative opportunities of the statesman. It is the legislator's task to frame a society which shall make the good life possible. Politics for Aristotle is not a struggle between individuals or classes for power, nor a device for getting done such elementary tasks as the maintenance of order and security without too great encroachments on individual liberty. The state is "a community of well-being in families and aggregations of families for the sake of a perfect and self-suffering life." The legislator is a craftsman whose material is society and whose aim is the good life.

SOCIETY AS EDUCATOR

In an early dialogue of Plato's *The Protagoras*, Socrates asks Protagoras why it is not as easy to find teachers of virtue as it is to find teachers of swordsmanship, riding, or any other art. Protagoras' answer is that there are no special teachers of virtue, because virtue is taught by the whole community. Plato and Aristotle both accept the view of moral education implied in this answer. In a passage of *The Republic*, Plato repudiates the notion that the sophists have a corrupting moral influence upon young men. The public themselves, he says, are the real sophists and the most complete and thorough educators. No private education can hold out against the irresistible force of public opinion and the ordinary moral standards of society. But that makes it all the more essential that public opinion and social environment should not be left to grow up as haphazard as they ordinarily do, but should be made by the wise legislator the expression of the good and be informed in all their details by his knowledge. The legislator is the only possible teacher of virtue.

THE BEST STATE

Aristotle's *Politics* is a handbook for the legislator, the expert who is to be called in when a state wants help. It is one of the most marked characteristics of Greek political theory that Plato and Aristotle think of the statesman as one who has knowledge of what ought to be done, and can help those who has power to control the forces of society. The desire of society for the statesman's advice is taken for granted. Plato in *The Republic* says that a good constitution is only possible when the ruler does not want to rule; where men contend for power, where they have not learnt to distinguish between the art of getting hold of the helm of state and the art of steering, which alone is statesmanship, true politics is impossible.

The best society is possible only in the best state. Therefore, education by society is education by state. Aristotle assumes the characteristic Platonic view that all men seek the good, and go wrong through ignorance, not through evil will, and so he naturally regards the state as a community which exists for the sake of the good life. It is in the state that common seeking after the good which is the profoundest truth about men and nature becomes explicit and knows itself. The state is for Aristotle prior to the family and the village, although it succeeds them in time, for only when the state with its conscious organisation is reached can man understand the secret of his past struggles after something he knew not what. If primitive society is understood in the light of its most perfect form, when the good after which all societies are seeking is realised in its perfection. Hence, for Aristotle as for Plato, the natural state or the state as such is the ideal state, and the ideal state is the starting point of political inquiry.

THE VALUE OF EDUCATION IN THE STATE

Aristotle assigns the paramount political importance to education. It is the great instrument by which the legislator can ensure that the future citizens of his state will share those common beliefs which make the state possible. The Greek with their small states had a far clearer apprehension than we can have of the dependence of a constitution upon the people who have to work it.

If the state is the organisation of men seeking a common good, power and political position must be given to those who can forward this end. This is the principle expressed in Aristotle's account of political justice, the principle of "tools to those who can use them." As the aim of the state is differently conceived, the qualifications for government will vary. In the ideal state power will be given to the men with most knowledge of the good; in other states to the men who are most truly capable of achieving that end which the citizens have set themselves to pursue. The most just distribution of political power is that in which there is least waste of political ability.

According to Aristotle, there are three qualifications necessary for those who fill the first departments in government: first of all, an affection for the established constitution; secondly, abilities every way completely equal to the business of their office; in the third, virtue and justice correspondent to the nature of that particular state they are placed in; for if justice is not the same in all states, it is evident that there must be different species thereof. To quote Aristotle, "But of all things which I have mentioned, that which contributes most to preserve the state is, what is now most despised, to educate your children for the state; for the most useful laws, and most approved by every statesman, will be of no service if the citizens are not accustomed to and brought up in the principles of the constitution; of a democracy, if that is by law established; of an oligarchy, if that is; for if there are bad morals in one man, there are in the city."[4] But to educate a child fit for the state, it must not be done in the manner which would please either those who have the power in an oligarchy or those who desire a democracy, but so as they may be able to conduct either of these forms of governments. But now the children of the magistrates in an oligarchy are brought up too delicately, and the children of the poor hardened with exercise and labour; so that they are both desirous of and able to promote innovations.

According to Aristotle, the virtue of a good citizen and good governor is the same as of a good man; and that every one before he commands should have first obeyed; it is the business of the legislator to consider how his citizens may be good men, what education is necessary to that purpose, and what is the final object of a good life.

OBJECTIVES OF EDUCATION

The soul of man may be divided into two parts; that which has reason in itself, and that which has not, but is capable of obeying its dictates. According to the virtues of these two parts, a man is said to be good. But of those virtues which are the ends, it will not be difficult for those to determine who adopt the division, already given. The inferior is always for the sake of the superior; and this is equally evident both in the work of art as well as in those of nature; but this is superior which has reason. Reason itself also is divided into two parts, the theoretic and the practical.

Now life is divided into labour and the rest, war and peace; and of what we do the objects are partly necessary and useful, partly noble; and we should give the same preference to those that we do to the different parts of the soul and its actions, as war to procure peace; labour, rest; and the useful, the noble. The politician, therefore, who composes a body of laws ought to extend his views to everything; the different parts of the soul and their actions; more particularly to those things which are of a superior nature and ends; and in the same manner, to the lives of men and their different actions. They ought to be fitted not both for labour and war, but rather for rest and peace; and also to do not what is necessary and useful, but rather what is fair and noble. It is to those objects that the education of the children ought to tend, and of all the youths who want instruction.

All the Grecian states which now seem best governed, and the legislators who founded those states, appear not to have framed their polity with a view to the best end, or to every virtue, in their laws and education; but eagerly to have attended to what is useful and productive of gain; and nearly of the same opinion with these are some persons who have written lately, who, by praising the Lacedaemonian state, show they approve of the intention of the legislator is making war and victory the end of his government.

REST AND PEACE

Moreover, neither should a city be thought happy, nor should a legislator be commended, because he has so trained the people as to conquer their neighbours; for in this there is a great inconvenience.[5] Reason indeed concurs with experience in showing that all the attention within the legislator pays to the business of war, and all other rules which he lays down, should have for their object rest and peace.[6]

Harmony as Object of Education

"As there is one end common to a man both as an individual and a citizen, it is evident that a good man and a good citizen must have the same object in view; it is evident that all the virtues which lead to rest are necessary; for, as we have often said, the end of war is peace, of labour, rest; but those virtues whose object is rest, and those also whose object is labour, are necessary for a liberal life and rest; for we want a supply of many necessary things that we may be at rest. A city therefore ought to be temperate, brave and patient; for according to the proverb, 'Rest is not for slaves;' but those who cannot bravely face danger are the slaves of those who attack them."[7] Bravery, therefore, and patience are necessary for labour, philosophy for rest, and temperance and justice in both; but these chiefly in time of peace and rest; for war obliges men to be just and temperate; but the enjoyment of pleasure, with the rest of peace, is more apt to produce insolence; those indeed who are easy in their circumstances, and enjoy everything that can make them happy, have great occasion for the virtues of temperance and justice. Thus if there are, as the poets tell us, any inhabitants in the happy isle, to these a higher degree of philosophy, temperance, and justice will he necessary, as they live at their ease in the full plenty of every sensual pleasure. It is evident, therefore, that these virtues are necessary in every state that would be happy or worthy; for he who is worthless can never enjoy real good, much less is he qualified to be at rest; but can appear good only by labour and being at war, but in peace and at rest the meanest of creatures.[8] Since there are greater goods than those which are valuable in themselves should be desired, rather than those virtues which are useful in war : but how and by what means this is to be acquired is now to be considered.

Aristotle assigned three causes on which it will depend: nature, custom and reason. He said, "It remains then that we determine which we shall first begin by the education, reason or custom, for these ought always to preserve the most entire harmony with each other; for it may happen that reason may err from the end proposed, and be corrected by custom."[9] In the first place, it is evident that in this as in other things, its beginning or production arises from some principle, and its end also arises from another principle, which is itself an end. Now, with man, reason and intelligence are the end of nature; his production, therefore, and his manners ought to be accommodated to both these. In the next place, as the soul and the body are two distinct things, and as the soul is divided into two parts, the reasoning and not-reasoning, with their habits, which are two in number, one belonging to each, namely, appetite and intelligence; and as the body is in production before the soul, so is the not-reasoning part of the soul before the reasoning; and this is evident; for anger, will, and desire are to be seen in children nearly as soon as they are born; but reason and intelligence spring up as they grow to maturity. According to Aristotle, "The body, therefore, necessarily demands our care before the soul; next the appetites, for the sake of the mind; the body for the sake of the soul."[10] Thus physical education should be subordinate to mental education though both are equally necessary.

EDUCATION OF THE CHILD

When a child is born, the strength of its body will depend greatly upon the quality of its food. People who desire that their children should acquire a warlike habit, feed them chiefly with milk, as being best accommodated to their bodies, but without wine, to prevent any distempers. Those notions which are natural to their age are very serviceable; and those should be prevented which make their limbs crooked. On account of their extreme ductility, some people use particular machines that their bodies may not be distorted. It is useful to allure them to the cold when they are very little; for this is very serviceable for their health; and to ensure them to the business of war; for whatever it is possible to acustom children to, it is best to accustom them to it at first, but to do it by degrees; besides, boys have naturally a habit of loving the cold, on account of the heat.

NO EDUCATION UP TO FIVE YEARS

According to Aristotle, "These, then and such like things ought to be the first object of our attention; the next age to this continues till the child is five years old; during which time it is best to teach him nothing at all, not even necessary labour, lest it should hinder his growth; but he should be accustomed to use so much motion as not to acquire a lazy habit of body; which he will get by various means and by play also; his play also ought to be neither illiberal nor too laborious, nor lazy."[11]

IMITATION THEORY OF PLAY

The governors and preceptors of children should take care what sort of tales and stories it may be proper for them to hear; for all these ought to pave the way for their future instruction; for which reason the generality of their play should be imitations of what they are afterwards to do seriously. They too do wrong who forbid by laws the disputes between boys and their quarrels, for they contribute to increase their growth; as they are a sort of exercise to the body. The struggles of the heart and the compression of the spirits give strength to those who labour, which happens to boys in their disputes. The preceptors also ought to have an eye upon their manner of life, and those with whom they converse; and to take care that they are never in the company of slaves.

HOME EDUCATION

At this time and till they are seven years old it is necessary that they should be educated at home. It is also very proper to banish, both from their hearing and sight, everything which is illiberal and the like. The legislator should banish every indecent expression out of the state; for from a permission to speak whatever is shameful, very quickly arises the doing of it, particularly with young people. Let them never speak nor hear any such thing. If it appears that any freeman has done or said anything that is forbidden before he is of age to be thought fit to partake of the common meals, let him be punished by disgrace and stripes. But if a person above that age does so, let him be treated as you would a slave, on account of his being infamous. As we forbid children speaking everything which is forbidden, it is necessary that he neither sees obscene stories nor pictures. The magistrates should take care that there are no statues or pictures of anything of this nature, except only of those gods to which the law allows persons of a certain age to pay their devotions, for themselves, their wives, and children. It should also be illegal for young persons to be present either at iambics or comedies before they are arrived at that age when they are allowed to partake of the pleasures of the table. To quote Aristotle, "Indeed a good education will preserve them from all the evils which attend on these things."[12]

According to Aristotle, what we meet with first pleases best; for which reason children should be kept strangers to everything which is bad, more particularly whatsoever is loose and offensive to good manners. When five years are accomplished, the two next may be very properly employed in being spectators of those exercises they will afterwards have to learn.

TWO PERIODS OF EDUCATION

According to Aristotle, there are two periods into which

education ought to be divided, according to the age of the child; the one is from his being seven years of age to the time of puberty; the other from puberty till he is twenty-one. Those who divide ages by the number seven are in general wrong; it is much better to follow the division of nature; for every art and every instruction is intended to complete what nature has left defective. Thus Aristotle, like the sages of India of his time, considered good *sanskaras* as the most important in the early education of the children. Today, when children are being indiscriminately exposed to all types of experiences, particularly through the media, it is a point worth consideration by those who are concerned with the education of the children. It is unfortunate that today, almost all over the world the contemporary pedagogues are neglecting this common wisdom of East and West.

EDUCATION BY MAGISTRATES

Aristotle says, "No one can doubt that the magistrate ought greatly to interest himself in the care of youth; for where it is neglected it is hurtful to the city, for every state ought to be governed according to its particular nature; for the form and manners of each government are peculiar to itself; and these, as they originally established it, so they usually still preserve it."[13] Universally, the best manners produce the best government. Besides, as in every business and art there are some things which men are to learn first and be made accustomed to, which are necessary to perform their several works, so it is evident that the same is necessary in the practice of virtue.

UNIFORM ONE SYSTEM OF EDUCATION

According to Aristotle, "As there is one end in view in every city, it is evident that education ought to be one and the same in each; and that this should be a common care, and not the individual's, as it now is, when every one takes care of his own children separately; and their instructions are particular also, each person teaching them as they please; but what ought to be engaged in, ought to be common to all."[14] Besides, no one ought to think that any citizen belongs to him in particular, but to the state in general; for each one is a part of the state, and it is the natural duty of each part to regard the good of the whole. Aristotle pointed to Lacedaemonians for they give the greatest attention to education, and make it public. "It is evident," he concludes, "then, that there should be laws concerning education, and that it should be public."[15]

CURRICULUM OF EDUCATION

According to Aristotle, "What education is, and how children ought to be instructed, is what should be well known; for there are doubts concerning the business of it, as all people do not agree in those things they would have a child taught, both with respect to their improvement in virtue and a happy life; nor is it clear whether the object of it should be to improve the reason or rectify the morals."[16]

Utility *vs.* Virtue

"From the present mode of education," continues Aristotle, "we cannot determine with certainty to which men incline, whether to instruct a child in what will be useful to him in life; or what tends to virtue, and what is excellent; for all these things have their separate defenders."[17] As to virtue, there are no particulars in which they all agree; for as all do not equally esteem all virtues, it reasonably follows that they will not cultivate the same. It is evident that what is necessary ought to be taught to all; but that which is necessary for one is not necessary for all; for there ought to be a distinction between the employment of a freeman and a slave. The first of these should be taught everything useful which will not make those who know it mean. According to Aristotle, "Every work is to be esteemed mean, and every art and every discipline which renders the body, to mind, or the understanding of freemen unfit for the habit and practice of virtue; for which reason all those arts which tend to deform the body are called mean, and all those employments which are exercised for gain; for they take off from the freedom of the mind and render it sordid."[18] There are also some liberal arts which are not improper for freemen to apply to in a certain degree; but to endeavour to acquire a perfect skill in them is exposed to the faults.

Aristotle points out that there are four things which it is usual to teach children — reading, gymnastic, exercises and music, to which (in the fourth place) some add painting. Reading and painting are both of them of singular use in life, and gymnastic exercises, as productive of courage. As to music some persons may doubt, as most persons now use it for the sake of pleasure; but those who originally made it part of education did it because, nature requires that we should not only be properly employed, but to be able to enjoy leisure honourably. According to Aristotle, though both labour and rest are necessary, yet the latter is preferable to the first; and by all means man ought to learn what he should do when at rest; for he ought not to employ that time at play; for then play would be the necessary business of his life. Play is more necessary for those who labour than those who are at rest : for as labour is attended with pain and continued exertion, it is necessary that play should be introduced, under proper regulations, as a medicine : for such an employment of the mind is a relaxation to it, and eases with pleasure. Now rest itself seems to partake the pleasure, of happiness, and an agreeable life : but this cannot be theirs who labour, but theirs who are at rest; for he who labours, labours for the sake of some end which he has not attained.

According to Aristotle, "Happiness is an end which all persons think is attended with pleasures and not with pain; but all persons do not agree in making this pleasure consist in the same thing; for each one has his particular standard, correspondent to his own habits; but the best man proposes the best pleasure, and that which arises from the noblest actions."[19] To live a life of rest there are some things which a man must learn and be instructed in. The object of this learning and this instruction centres in their acquisition. The learning and instruction which is given for labour has for its object other things. The ancients made music a part of education; not as a thing necessary, for it is not of that nature, nor as a thing useful, as reading, in the common course of life, or for managing of a family, or for learning anything as useful in public life. Painting also seems useful to enable a man to judge more accurately of the productions of the finer arts; nor is it like the gymnastic exercises, which contribute to health and strength; for neither of these things do we see produced by music. The employment of our rest, they had in view who introduced it. It is a proper employment for freeman. It is evident, then, that there is a certain education in which a child may be instructed, not as useful nor as necessary, but as noble and liberal. We have the testimony of the ancients in our favour, by what they have delivered down upon education — for music makes this plain. Moreover, it is necessary to instruct children in what is useful, not only on account of its being useful in itself, as, for instance, to learn to read, but also as the means of acquiring other different sorts of instruction. Thus, they should be instructed in painting, not only to prevent their committing mistakes in purchasing pictures, or in buying or selling of vases, but rather as it makes them judges of the beauties of the human form. According to Aristotle, "To be always hunting after the profitable ill agrees with great and freeborn souls."[20] Whether a boy should be first taught morals or reasoning, and whether his body or his understanding should be first cultivated, it is plain that boys should be put under the care of the different masters of the gymnastic arts, both to form their bodies and teach them their exercises.

PHYSICAL EDUCATION

Aristotle criticised those states which took greatest care of their children's education by bestowing their chief attention on wrestling, because it both prevents the growth of the body and hurts the form of it. The Lacedaemonians made their children fierce by painful labour, as chiefly useful to inspire them with courage; though, this is neither the only thing nor the principal thing necessary to attend to; and even with respect to this they may not thus attain their end. Aristotle pointed out, "We do not find either in other animals, or other nations, that courage necessarily attends to the most cruel, but rather the milder, and those who have the dispositions of lion; for there are many people who are eager both to kill men and to devour human flesh, as the Achaeans and Meniochi in Pontus, and many others in Asia, some of whom are as bad, others worse than those who indeed live by tyranny, but are men of no courage."[21] The Lacedaemonians did not acquire their superiority by training their youth to these exercises, but because those who were disciplined opposed those who were not disciplined at all. What is fair and honourable ought then to take place in education of what is fierce and cruel; for it is not a wolf, nor any other wild beast, which will brave any noble danger, but rather a good man. According to Aristotle, those who permit boys to engage too earnestly in these exercises, while they do not take care to instruct them in what is necessary to do, to speak the real truth, render them mean and vile, accomplished only in one duty of a citizen, and in every other respect, as reason evinces, good of nothing. Gymnastic exercises are useful during youth. It is very proper to go through a course of those which are most gentle, omitting violent diet and painful exercises as they may prevent the growth of the body. In support of this argument, Aristotle points out that amongst the Olympic candidates one can scarcely find two or three who have gained a victory both when boys and men; because the necessary exercises they went through when young deprived them of their strength. When they have allotted three years from the time of puberty to other parts of education, they are then of a proper age to submit to labour and a regulated diet. According to Aristotle, "It is impossible for the mind and the body both to labour at the same time, as they are productive of contrary evils to each other; the labour of the body preventing the progress of the mind, and the mind of the body."[22]

EDUCATION IN MUSIC

About the purpose of education in music Aristotle points out, "It is no easy matter to distinctly point our what power it has, not on what accounts one should apply it, whether as an amusement and refreshment, as sleep or wine; as these are nothing serious, but pleasing, and the killers of care, as Euripides says : for which reason they class in the same order and use for the same purpose all these, namely, sleep, wine, and music, to which some add dancing; or shall we rather suppose that music tends to be productive of virtue, having a power, as the gymnastic exercises have, to form the body in a certain way, to influence the manners so as to accustom its professors to rejoice rightly? or shall we say, that is of any service in the conduct of life, and an assistant to prudence? for this also is a third property which has been attributed to it."[23] According to Aristotle, the boys should not be instructed in music as play because for those who learn don't play, for to learn it is rather troublesome. Neither is it proper to permit boys at their age to enjoy perfect leisure; for to cease to improve is by no means fit for what is as yet imperfect. It may be thought that the earnest attention of boys in music is for the sake of that amusement they will enjoy when they come to be men and completely formed. But if this is the case, why are they themselves to learn it, and not follow the practice of the kings of the Medes and Persians, who enjoy the pleasure of music by hearing others play, and being shown its beauties by them; for of necessity those must be better skilled therein who make this science their particular study and business, than those who have only spent so much time at it as was sufficient just to learn the principles of it. But if this is a reason for a child's being taught music, they ought also to learn the art of cookery, which is absurd. The same doubt occurs if music has a power of improving the manners; for why should they on this account themselves learn it, and not reap every advantage of regulating the passions or forming a judgment on the merits of the performance by hearing others. The same reasoning may be applied if music is supposed to be the amusement of those who live an elegant and easy life, why should they learn themselves, and not rather enjoy the benefit of other's skill.

MUSIC FOR HARMONY

According to Aristotle, the first question is, whether music is or is not to make a part of education? and of those three things which have been assigned as its proper employment, which is the right? Is it to instruct, to amuse, or to employ the vacant hours of those who live at rest? or may not all three be properly allotted to it? for it appears to partake of them all; for play is necessary for relaxation, and relaxation is pleasant, as it is a medicine for that uneasiness which arises from labour. It is admitted also that a happy life must be an honourable one, and a pleasant one too, since happiness consists in both these; and music is one of the most pleasing things, whether alone or accompanied with a voice, for which reason it is justly admitted into every company and every happy life, as having the power of inspiring joy. From this any one may suppose that it is necessary to instruct young persons in music; for all those pleasures which are harmless are not only conducive to the final end of life, but serve also as relaxation; and, as men are but rarely in the attainment of that final end, they often cease from their labour and apply to amusement, with no further view than to acquire the pleasure attending it. It is therefore useful to enjoy such pleasures as these. There are some persons who make play and amusement their end, and probably that end has some pleasure annexed to it, but while men seek the one they accept the other for it; because there is some likeness in human actions to the end; for the end is pursued for the sake of nothing else attends it, but for itself only; and pleasures like these are sought for, not on account of what follows them, but on account of what has gone beiore them, as labour and grief; for which reason they seek for happiness in these sort of pleasures; and that this is the reason any one may easily perceive.

That music should be pursued, not on this account only, but also as it is very serviceable during the hours of relaxation from labour, probably no one doubts. Music naturally gives pleasure, therefore the use of it is agreeable to all ages and all dispositions. It fills the soul with enthusiasm; which is an affection of the soul and strongly agitates the disposition. In poetry and music there are imitations of manners. Different harmonies differ from each other so much by nature, that those who hear them are differently affected, and are not in the same disposition of mind when one is performed as when another is; the one, for instance, occasions grief and contracts the soul; other often the mind, and as it were dissolve the heart; others fix it in a firm and settled state, while others fill the soul with enthusiasm, as has been well described by those who have written philosophically upon this part of education; for they bring examples of what they advance from the things themselves. The same holds true with respect of rhythm; some act more violently, others more liberally. Thus it is evident that music has an influence over the disposition of the mind, and it can fascinate it variously and if it can do this, most certainly it is what the youth ought to be instructed in. The learning of music is particularly adapted to young disposition; for at their time of life they do not willingly attend to anything which is not agreeable. Music is naturally one of the most agreeable things; and there seems to be a certain connection between harmony and rhythm. Some wise men hold the soul itself to be harmony; others, that it contains it.

INSTRUMENTAL MUSIC

Is it proper that children should be taught to sing, and play upon any instrument? Now, it is well known that it makes a great deal of difference when you would qualify any one in any art, for the person himself to learn the practical part of it; for it is a thing very difficult, if not impossible, for a man to be a good judge of what he himself cannot do. It is also very necessary that children should have some employment which will amuse them; for at their age they cannot sit still. Instruction ought to be their rattle. Infants as they grow up, should be so taught music as to be able to practise it. In the first place, it is necessary for them to practise that they may be judges of the art. This should be done when they are young. But when they are grown older the practical part may be dropped; while they will still continue judges of what is excellent in the art, and take a proper pleasure therein, from the knowledge they acquired of it in their youth.

As to the censure which some persons, including Plato, throw upon music, as something mean and low, Aristotle asks us to consider how far we propose that those who are to be educated to become good citizens should be instructed in this art, and what music and what rhythms they should be acquainted with; and also what instruments they should play upon; for in these there is probably a difference. It must be admitted, that in some cases nothing can prevent music being attended, to a certain degree, with the bad effects which are ascribed to it. It is therefore clear that the learning of it should never prevent the business of riper years; nor render the body effeminate, and unfit for the business of war or the state; but it should be practised by the young, judged of by the old. According to Aristotle, "That children may learn music properly, it is necessary that they should not be employed in those parts of it which are the objects of dispute between the masters in that science; nor should they perform such pieces as are wondered at from the difficulty of their execution; and which, from being first exhibited in the public games, are now become a part of education; but let them learn so much of it as to be able to receive proper pleasure from excellent music and rhythms; and not that only which music must make all animals feel, and also slaves and boys, but more."[24]

PLAYING AT FLUTE FORBIDDEN

They should never be taught to play upon the flute, or any other instrument which requires great skill, as the harp or the like, but on such as will make them good judges of music, or any other instruction. Besides, the flute is not a moral instrument, but rather one that will inflame the passion. It is, therefore, rather to be used when the soul is to be animated than when instruction is intended. According to Aristotle, "There is something in flute which is quite contrary to what education requires; as the player on the flute prevented from speaking: for which reason our forefathers very properly forbade the use of it to youth and freemen, no one in particular, but endeavouring to collect them"[25] At Lacedaemon the choregus himself played on the flute; and it was so common at Athens that almost every freeman understood it, as is evident from the tablet which Thrasippus dedicated when he was choregus; but afterwards they rejected it as dangerous; having become better judges of what tended to promote virtue and what did not. For the same reason many of the ancient instruments were thrown aside, as the dulcimer and the lyre; as also those which were to inspire those who played on them with pleasure, and which required a nice finger and great skill to play well on. According to Aristotle, "What the ancients tell us, by way of fable, of the flute is indeed very rational; namely, that after Minerva had found it, she threw it away; nor are they wrong who say that the goddess disliked it for deforming the face of him who played thereon."[26] According to Aristotle, it is more probable that she rejected it as the knowledge thereof contributed nothing to the improvement of the mind. In Greece Minerva was the inventress of arts and sciences. Aristotle disapproved of a child's being taught to understand instruments, and to play like a master which should be confined to those who are candidates for the prize in that science; for they play not to improve themselves in virtue, but to please those who hear them, and gratify their importunity. Therefore, the practice of flute is unfit for freemen; but it should be confined to those who are paid for doing it.

ROLE OF HARMONY AND RHYTHM IN EDUCATION

Aristotle entered into an inquiry concerning harmony and rhythm; whether all sorts of these are to be employed in education, or whether some peculiar ones are to be selected; and also whether we should give the same directions to those who are engaged in music as part of education, whether there is something different from these two. Now as all music consists in melody and rhythm, we ought not to be unacquainted with the power which each of these have in education; and whether we should rather choose music in which melody prevails or rhythm.

Melody has been rightly divided by some philosophers, into moral, practical, and that which fills the mind with enthusiasm. They also allot to each of those a particular kind of harmony which naturally corresponds therewith. Music should not be applied to one purpose only, but many; both for instruction and purifying the soul and, in the third place, as an agreeable manner of spending the time and a relaxation from the uneasiness of the mind. It is evident that all harmonies are to be used; but not for all purposes; but the most moral in education; but to please the ear, when others play, the most active and enthusiastic; for that passion which is to be found very strong in some souls is to be met with also in all; but the difference in different persons consists in its being in a less or greater degree, as pity, fear, and enthusiasm also; which latter is so powerful in some as to overpower the soul; and yet we see those persons, by the application of sacred music to soothe their mind, rendered as sedate and composed as if they had employed the art of the physician; and this must necessarily happen to the compassionate, the fearful, and all those who are subdued by their passions, admit of the same cure, and are restored to tranquillity with pleasure.

In the same manner, all music which has the power of purifying the soul affords a harmless pleasure to man. Such, therefore, should be the harmony and such the music which those who contend with each other in the theatre should exhibit; but as the audience is composed of two sorts of people, the free and the well-instructed, the rude, the mean mechanics, and hired servants, and a long collection of the like, there must be some music and some spectacles to please and soothe them; for as their minds are as it were perverted from their natural habits, so also is there an unnatural harmony, and overcharged music, which is accommodated to their taste; but what is according to nature gives pleasure to every one, therefore those who are to contend upon the theatre should be allowed to use this species of music. But in education ethic melody and ethic harmony should be used, which is the Doric, as we have already said, or any other which those philosophers who are skinful in that music which is to be employed in education shall approve of. But Socrates, in Plato's *The Republic*, is very wrong when he permits only the Phrygian music to be used as well as the Doric, particularly as amongst other instruments he banishes the flute; for the Phrygian music has the same power in harmony as the flute has amongst the instruments; for they are both pathetic and raise the mind; and this the practice of the poets proves; for in their bacchanal songs, or whenever they describe any violent emotions of the mind, the flute is the instrument they chiefly use; and the Phrygian harmony is most suitable to these subjects. Now, that the dithyrambic measure is Phrygian is allowed by general consent; and those who are conversant in studies of this sort bring many proofs of it; as, for instance, when Philogenus endeavoured to compose dithyrambic music for Doric harmony, he naturally fell back again into Phrygian, as being fittest for that purpose; as every one indeed agrees, that the Doric music is most serious, and fittest to inspire courage; and as we always commend the middle as being between the two extremes, and the Doric has this relation with respect to other harmonies, it is evident that is what the youth ought to be instructed in.

There are two things to be taken into consideration, both what is possible and what is proper; everyone then should chiefly endeavour to attain those things which contain both these qualities; but this is to be regulated by different times of life; for instance, it is not easy for those who are advanced in years to sing such pieces of music as require very high notes, for nature points out to them those which are gentle and require little strength of voice for which reason some who are skilful in music justly find fault with Socrates for forbidding the youth to be instructed in gentle harmony; as if, like wine, it would make them drunk, whereas the effect of that is to render men bacchanals, and not make them languid; these therefore are what should employ those who are grown old. "Moreover, if there is any harmony which is proper for a child's age, as being at the same time elegant and instructive, as the Lydian of all others seems chiefly to be — These then are as it were the three boundaries of education, moderation, possibility, and decorum."[27]

REFERENCES

1. Thilly, Frank *History of Philosophy,* p. 118.
2. Gomperz, *Greek Thinkers*, pp. 18-19.

3. Zeller, *Outlines of the History of Greek Philosophy*, p. 158.
4. Aristotle, *Politics*, translated by William Elis (London : J.M. Dent & Sons Ltd., 1912), p. 166.
5. *Ibid.*, 229.
6. *Ibid.*, 230.
7. *Ibid.*
8. *Ibid.*, 237.
9. *Ibid.*
10. *Ibid.*, 232.
11. *Ibid.*, p. 235.
12. *Ibid.*, p. 236.
13. *Ibid.*, p. 238.
14. *Ibid.*
15. *Ibid.*
16. *Ibid.*, p. 239.
17. *Ibid.*
18. *Ibid.*
19. *Ibid.*
20. *Ibid.*, pp. 241-42.
21. *Ibid.*, p. 242.
22. *Ibid.*, p. 243.
23. *Ibid.*, p. 244.
24. *Ibid.*, p. 249.
25. *Ibid.*
26. *Ibid.*, p. 250.
27. *Ibid.*, p. 253.

3

JOHN AMOS COMENIUS

(1592-1670)

Plato and Aristotle had confirmed their attention to the training of the governing classes of the community. Until the time of Comenius, idealists like Moore hazarded the suggestion that 'all in their childhood be instructed in learning...in their own native tongue.'[1] Comenius proposed to teach 'all things to all men,' but set about planning a universal system of education in a practical fashion devising methods of teaching which would hasten the attainment of his ideal. He even prepared school books to illustrate how his principles should be applied in practice. It was not on the grounds of an abstract political principle like the equality of man that he based his belief. He advocated that education should be accessible to all rather by reason of the infinite possibilities in human nature and of the uncertainty about the position to which providence might call this or that man. Such a faith in the universal education of the people could at that time be based only on the religious ground. The idea of universalising education proved more difficult of realisation than could have been foreseen by Comenius. As M. Spinka says about Comenius, "He became an educational reformer more by accident than by primary design; and it would be doing him less than justice if we were to fail to recognise his primary and dominant life-motive."[2]

THE LABYRINTH

Commenius exerted to succour his persecuted and exiled people by his endeavour to assuage the bitter dissensions between the factions of the Reformed Church. His most influential gift to the religious life of his nation was *The Labyrinth of the World and the Paradise of the Heart,* the supplementary title of which reads — "A book that clearly shows that this world and all matters concerning it are nothing but confusion and giddiness, pain and toil, deceit and falsehood, misery and anxiety, and lastly, disgust of all things and despair; but he who remains in his own dwelling within his heart, opening it to the Lord God alone, will obtain true and full peace of mind and joy."[3]

Subject Matter of *The Labyrinth*

The Labyrinth was in many respects analogous to Bunyan's *Pilgrim's Progress*. It became a classic in Czech literature. It was one of the great books of mystical devotion. The sections in *The Labyrinth* having educational significance are those in which Comenius described the current pedagogical practice and what he regards ought to be the practice. "I speak not of their pouches" he said, "but of their skins which had to suffer, for fists, canes, sticks, birch rods struck them on their cheeks, heads, backs and posteriors till blood streamed forth, and they were almost entirely covered with stripes, scars, spots and weals."[4] In the ideal state, the paradise of the heart, however, Comenius described how he found "a few learned men, who, contrary to the customs of the world, surpassed the others in humility as greatly as they did in learning, and they were sheer gentleness and kindness. It befalls that I spoke to one of them, from whom it was thought to earthly learning was concealed, yet he bore himself as a most simple man, sighing deeply over his stupidity and ignorance. The knowledge of languages they held in slight value, if the knowledge of wisdom was not added to it. For languages, they said, give not wisdom, but have that purpose only that by means of them we can converse with many and diverse inhabitants of the terrestrial globe, be they alive or dead. Therefore, not he, they said, who can speak many languages, but he who can speak of useful things, is learned. Now they call useful things all God's works, and they said that arts are of some use for the purpose of understanding Him; but they also say that the true fountain of knowledge is Holy Writ, and the Holy Ghost our teacher, and that the purpose of all true knowledge is Christ, He who was crucified."[5]

PANSOPHISM

Comenius' efforts for educational reform were inspired by religious motives. However, the great interests of his life, apart from religion, lay in a scheme of universal knowledge or pansophism. This influenced and sometimes diverted him from his educational activities. Pansophism is not mere encyclopaedism. In *The Permanent Values in Education,* Kenneth Rishmond pointed out, "Encyclopaedic teaching is neither practicable nor desirable; pansophic teaching is both. The one aims at making the learner an inexhausible mind of information upon every subject, the other would make him capable of wisdom in his regard for any subject and able to see any subject in relation to others and to general principles."[6] Pansophism is not 'the correlation of sciences in unity' as Laurie purposes in his Comenius. Correlation is, after all, a somewhat artificial and external process. Pansophism is best understood when expressed in modern terms as recognition of the organic conception of knowledge — the 'flower in the Crannied well.' According to Comenius himself, Pansophism is "an accurate anatomy of the universe, dissecting the veins and limbs of all things in such a way that there shall be nothing that is not seen, and that each part shall appear in its place and without confusion."[7] The purpose of Pansophism as Comenius explains in *The Way of Light,*[8] is not so much to make men learned as to make them wise, to give them understanding of their own ends and of the end of all things.

Pansophic conception reflects the influence of Bacon. It recalls the *New Atlantis* rather than the scientific method of the Advancement of Learning or the *Novum Organum*. In the *New Atlantis* the central feature is Salomon's House, 'which house or college is the very eye of the kingdom.' Its foundation is the embodiment of the scientific spirit which Bacon hoped might bring happiness to humanity. Salomon's House is a great laboratory equipped with all sort of scientific instruments. Associated with it is an organised army of scientific investigators. All the processes of nature are there artificially reproduced. The results are made to serve mankind. Comenius failed to appreciate the value of experiment in science on which Bacon insisted. He believed that the progress of humanity could be materially advanced by the collection of all available knowledge of God, nature and art, and by its reduction, to a system called Pansophia or Universal Wisdom.

The Great Didactic[9] belongs to the earlier period of Comenius' life. This period was religious rather than pansophic. According to Adamson, 'The Great Didactic setting forth the whole Art of Teaching all Things to all Men,' nevertheless reveals 'the desire for omniscience' which is very rarely absent from the seventeenth century writers.[10] The subtitle formulates Comenius' democratic attitude. It runs, "A certain inducement to found such schools in all the Parishes, Town and Villages of every Christian Kingdom that entire youth of both sexes, none being excepted, shall quickly, pleasantly and thoroughly become learned in the sciences, pure in Morals, trained to Piety, and in this manner instructed in all things necessary for the present and for the future life".

Educational Revolution

It is evident from the complaint about the condition of the schools of their day common to all the pedagogical writers of the period that a reorganisation of educational institutions and a revolution in educational methods were urgent.

Conditions of Contemporary Schools

About these schools Comenius wrote, "They are the terror of boys and the slaughter houses of minds — places where ten or more years are spent in learning what might be acquired in one, where what ought to be poured in gently is violently forced in and beaten in, where what ought to be put clearly and perspicaciously is presented in a confused and intricate way, as if it were a collection of puzzles — places where minds are fed on words."[11]

Education for Both Boys and Girls

In *The Great Didactic* Comenius dismissed existing schools more succinctly as 'terrors for boys and shambles for their intellects.' In accordance with the ideal of the universal school expressed in the subtitle of *The Great Didactic* Comenius wanted to establish a system of education that all the young, "not the children of the rich or of the powerful only but all alike, boys and girls, both noble and ignoble, rich and poor, in all cities and towns, villages and hamlets, should be sent to school. Let none therefore be excluded unless God has denied him sense and intelligence."[12] About the education of girls, Comenius said, "They are endowed with equal sharpness of mind and capacity for knowledge, and they are able to attain the highest positions since they have often been called by God Himself to rule over nations. Why, therefore, should we admit them to the alphabet, and afterwards drive them away from books?"

IMPORTANCE OF SCHOOL EDUCATION

According to Comenius, school education is preferable to home education; schools are necessary since it is seldom that parents have adequate ability or necessary leisure to instruct their children. To quote his words, "And although there might be parents with leisure to educate their own children, it is nevertheless better that the young should be taught together and in large classes, since better results and more pleasure are to be obtained when one pupil serves as an example and a stimulus for another. For to do what we see others do, to go where others go, to follow those who are ahead of us, and to keep in front of those who are behind us is the course of action to which we are all most naturally inclined. Young children especially are always more easily led and ruled by example than by precept. If you give them a precept, it makes little impression; if you point out that others are doing something they imitate without being told to do so."[13] Comenius was an advocate of common school for all.

He said, "We wish all men to be trained in all the virtues, especially in modesty, sociability and politeness, and it is therefore undesirable to create class distinctions at such an early age, or to give some children the opportunity of considering their own lot with satisfaction and that of others with scorn."[14]

SCHOOL ORGANISATION

Comenius wanted to organise schools on the following plan : a mother or nursery school for children up to the age of six, a vernacular or primary school in every village for pupils of six to twelve, a Latin or secondary school in every city for pupils of twelve to eighteen, and a university in every kingdom or province for youths from eighteen to twenty-four preparing for the professions. According to Comenius, promotion was to be given by ability.

When boys are only six years old, it is too early to determine their vocation in life, or whether they are more suited for learning or for manual labour. At this age neither mind nor the inclinations are sufficiently developed. "The admission to Latin school should not be reserved for the sons of rich men, nobles and magistrates, as if these were the only boys who would ever be able to fill similar positions. The wind blows where it will, and does not always begin to blow at a fixed time."[15] University entrance is to be more stringently restricted. "The studies will progress with ease and success if only select intellects, the flower of mankind, attempt them. The rest had better turn their attention to more suitable occupations, such as agriculture, mechanics or trade."[16]

Defects of Existing Schools

Comenius was distressed by the lack of internal organisation of the existing schools. Among the defects of the existing schools which Comenius pointed out and which he diagnosed were that each school, even each teacher, used a different method, that one procedure was followed in one language and another in a second, and even in the same subject the method was so varied that the pupil scarcely understood the way in which he was expected to learn. There was no method by which instruction could be given to all the pupils in a class at the same time. The individual alone was taught.[17]

To remedy these defects Comenius proposed that there should only be one teacher in each school or at any rate in each class; only one author should be used for each subject studied; the same exercises should be given to the whole class; all subjects and languages should be taught by the same method; everything should be taught thoroughly, briefly and pithily; all things that are naturally connected ought to be taught in combination; every subject should be taught in definitely graded steps, that the work of one day may thus, expand that of the previous day, and lead up to that of the morrow; and finally, everything that is useless should be invariably discarded.[18]

Besides making instruction more methodical, Comenius also made it more agreeable to the pupil. He suggested that the school should be situated in a quiet spot, far from noise and distraction.[19] He said, "The school itself should be a pleasant place, and attractive to the eye both within and without. Within, the room should be bright and clean, and its walls should be ornamented by pictures. These should be either portraits of celebrated men, geographical maps, historical plans, or other ornaments."[20] "Without, there should be an open place to walk and to play in for this is absolutely necessary for children, and there should also be a garden attached, into which scholars may be allowed to go from time to time and where they may feast their eyes on trees, flowers and plants. If this be done, boys will in all probability go to school with as much pleasure as to fairs, where they always hope to see and hear something new."[21]

Education of Senses

Comenius reiterated the principle that the child should be first instructed in things before being taught to express them in language, that everything should be first learned through the medium of the senses.[22] Men must, as far as possible, be taught to become wise by studying the heavens, the earth, oaks, and beeches, but not by studying books; that is to say, they must learn to know and investigate the things themselves, and not the observations that other people have made about the things. We shall thus tread in the footsteps of the wise man of old, if each of us obtains his knowledge from the originals, from things themselves, and from no other sources.[23] Echoing Bacon Comenius added, "That no information should be imparted on the grounds of bookish authority, but should be authorised by actual demonstration for the senses and to the intellect."

The common school for all pupils from six to twelve years of age necessitates that the teaching of other languages should be carried on through the mother tongue.[24] Direct instruction in the mother tongue itself should also be given. To quote Comenius, "To attempt to reach a foreign language before the mother tongue has been learned is as irrational as to teach a body to ride before he can walk. Cicero declared that he could not teach elocution to those who were unable to speak, and, in the same way, my method confesses its inability to teach Latin to those who are ignorant of their mother tongue, since the one paves the way for the other. Finally, what I have in view is an education in the objects that surround us, and a brief survey of this education can be obtained from books written in the mother tongue which embody a list of the things that exist in the external world. This preliminary survey will render the acquisition of Latin far easier, for it will only be necessary to adapt a new nomenclature to objects."[25]

CURRICULUM

Comenius' curriculum included "all those subjects which are able to make a man wise, virtuous and pious."[26] He required that every pupil should have a universal insight into things, and the qualification which he adds is apparent rather than real. As he said, "But do not, therefore, imagine that we demand for all men a knowledge (that is to say, an exact or deep knowledge) of all the arts and sciences. It is the principles, the causes, and the uses of all the most important things in existence that we wish all men to learn; all, that is to say, who are sent into the world to be actors as well as spectators. For we must take strong and vigorous measures that no man in his journey through life may encounter anything unknown to him that he cannot pass sound judgement upon it and turn it to its proper use without error."[27]

PRINCIPLES OF ORDER

Comenius assumed that all the errors of the past could be avoided and all his aims achieved by the adoption of the principles of order. Order was education's, as well as heaven's, first law. Accordingly, Comenius contended that the art of teaching demands nothing more than the skilful arrangement of time, of the subjects taught and of the method. Comenius failed to recognise the importance of the teacher in education. He assumed that this could be conveyed to all. Thus, he added, "As soon as we succeed in finding the proper method it will be no harder to teach school boys in any number desired that with the help of the printing press to cover a thousand sheets daily with the neatest writing."[28]

1. Follow Nature. Comenius believed that the right order, or proper method, can be secured if we 'follow nature.' Thus, he declared, "That order which is the dominating principle in the art of teaching all things to all men, should be, and can be borrowed from no other source but the operations of nature. As soon as this principle is thoroughly secured, the processes of art will proceed as easily and as spontaneously as those of nature."[29] For Comenius, 'following nature' consists in adducing analogies from natural processes in support of preconceived and independently acquired principles. The analogies are in many instances quite fanciful and lend no authority to the maxims of method which are supposed to be based on them. Thus, 'Nature observes as suitable time.'

For example, a bird that wishes to multiply its species, does not set about it in winter, when everything is stiff with cold, nor in summer, when everything is parched and withered by the heat; nor yet in autumn, when the vital force of all creatures declines with the sun's declining rays, and a new winter with hostile mien is approaching; but in spring, when the sun brings back life and strength to all.

2. Imitation. In the same way the gardener takes care to do nothing out of season.

3. Deviation. In direct opposition to this principle, twofold error is committed in schools :

(i) The right time for mental exercise is not chosen.

(ii) The exercises are not properly divided, so that all advance may be made through the several stages needful, without any omission.

4. Ratification. We conclude, therefore, that :

(i) The education of men should be commenced in the springtime of life, that is to say, in boyhood.

(ii) The morning hours are the most suitable for study (for here again the morning is the equivalent of spring).

(iii) All the subjects that are to be learned should be arranged so as to suit the age of the students, that nothing which is beyond their comprehension be given them to learn.

TEACHING METHODS

Among the following statements of Comenius may be found some of the traditional maxims of teaching method :

1. Easy to Difficult. 'Proceed from what is easy to what is more difficult.'

2. General to Particular. Instead of the maxim 'Proceed from the particular to the general.'

3. The Principle of Correlation or Integration of Studies. That is implied in the statement; 'great stress (should) be laid on the points of resemblance between cognate subjects;' and 'all things that are naturally connected ought to be taught in combination.'[30]

4. The Inductive Method of Teaching. This is expressed thus : [31] 'It is necessary that examples come before rules.'

5. Doctrine of Interest. It is anticipated in such remarks as 'The desire to know and to learn should be excited in the boy in every possible manner.'[32] Every study should be commenced in such a manner.[33]

6. Principles of Development. Although Comenius' own psychology was of the most primitive type, he anticipated the psychological principle of Pestalozzi when he affirmed that nothing should be taught to the young, unless it is not only permitted but actually demanded by their age and mental strength.

NOT NATURALISM

The misapplication of natural analogies by Comenius has misled some writers[34] into regarding him as a naturalist in philosophy. There is no doubt that Comenius was influenced by the new scientific movement initiated by Bacon. This, however, doe not justify the ascription of naturalist to him. In his *History of Western Education* Boyd is nearer the truth when he affirms that the religious bent of Comenius' mind inclined him to lay the main stress on the idealistic view of mental development.[35] Spinka clinches the issue by designating Comenius 'the incurable idealist.'[36]

CRITICAL EVALUATION

The value of Comenius' principles must be estimated independently of the analogies from nature given in support of them. The procedure he adopts while apparently securing uniformity in presentation actually results in a most unsystematic arrangement of the principles of school organisation and of educational method. His claim to present an apriori system is far from justified. His criticism of his predecessors' collections of a posteriori precepts are not inapplicable to his own work.

COMPARISON WITH JESUITS

Some of the principles and methods recommended by Comenius are common to him and to the Jesuits, the success of whose practices he cited in support of the procedures he advocated.[37] He advised that care should be exercised in the selection of texts put into pupils' hands. He maintained that the books which the scholars use should be such as can rightly be termed sources of wisdom, virtue and piety. He deplores the fact that more caution has not been exercised in the matter. *The Ratio Studiorum* instructs the Provincial to secure that school books which might do harm to virtue or good morals should be withheld from pupils till the offensive passages are expurgated. The professors of the Lower Studies are advised to refrain from introducing words prejudicial to good morals, not only to abstain from expounding these but also to deter pupils from reading them out of school as far as possible. Comenius also recommended the use of epitomes and criticised their use by the Jesuits.[38] The following extracts from *The Great Didactic* reads almost like a translation of the Jesuit regulations, "If the scholars are to be interested, care must be taken to make the method palatable, so that everything, no matter how serious, may be placed before them in a familiar and attractive manner: in the form of dialogue, for instance, by pitting the boys against one another to answer and explain riddling questions, comparisions and fables ...". The civil authorities and the managers of schools can kindle the zeal of the scholars by being present at public performance such as declarations, deputations, and promotions, and by praising the industrious ones and giving them small presents without respect of person. Even emulation is commended by Comenius as 'by far the best stimulus'[39] with school pupils.

SCHOOL DISCIPLINE

Comenius held enlightened views on school discipline. His recommendations followed the principles enunciated by Quintilian on this subject. Thus, he affirmed that no blows be given for lack of readiness to learn for, if the pupils do not learn readily, this is the fault of no one but the teacher, who either does not know how to make his pupil receptive of knowledge or does not take the trouble to do so.[40] In his chapter 'Of School

Discipline,' Comenius said, "A musician does not strike his lyre a blow with his fist or with a stick, nor does he throw it against the wall, because it produces a discordant sound; but setting to work on scientific principles, he tunes it and gets it into order. Just such a skinful and sympathetic treatment is necessary to instill a love of learning into the minds of our pupils, and any other procedure will only convert their idleness into antipathy and their lack of industry into downright stupidity."

TEXTBOOKS

Comenius felt the need of suitable textbooks. Like the other educators of his time and in spite of the prominence he assigned to the teaching of the vernacular, Comenius was condemned to devote attention to the teaching of languages, especially of Latin. Here he met with his greatest practical success. The manuals he prepared to facilitate the learning of Latin won ready acceptance. His *Janua Linguarum Reserata* was the most celebrated school book ever published. His *Orbis Pictus* was one of the earliest to introduce visual aids.

Though there is much repetition and contradiction among the principles of Comenius, but his writings evince a sincere sympathy with childhood. They start with an earnest aspiration to make education available to all, to lighten the drudgery of learning for the child, and to introduce into schools a humane treatment of the pupil. It has even been claimed by Kandel[41] that the establishment of the United Nations Educational, Scientific and Cultural Organisation marks the culmination of a movement for the creation of an international agency for education which began with the following statement in Comenius, "Universal harmony and peace must be secured for the whole human race. By peace and harmony, however, I mean not that external peace between rulers and peoples among themselves, but an internal peace of mind inspired by a system of ideas and feelings." To guarantee the stability of the world there must be 'some universal rededication of minds' beginning in the schools of each nation.

REFERENCES

1. *Utopia*, 182.
2. Cf. M. Spinka, *John Amos Comenius*, p. 32.
3. John Amo Komensky, *The Labyrinth of the World and the Paradise of the Heart*, edited and translated by Count Lutzow (London : Swan Sonnenschein & Co., 1901).
4. Count Latzow's translation, pp. 116-17.
5. *The Lubyrinth*, pp. 335-36.
6. K. Richmond, *op. cit.* (London : Constable & Co. Ltd., 1917), p. 36.
7. Laurie, S.S., *John Amos Comenius* (Cambridge University Press, 1899), p. 20.
8. Comenius, John Amos, *The Way of Light*, Translated into English with Introduction by E.T. Campagnac (The University Press of Liverpool, 1938), pp. 148-51.
9. Keatinge, N.W., *The Great Didactic of John Amos Comenius* (London : A & C. Blake, 1938).
10. Adamson, J.W., *Pioneers of Modern Education* (Cambridge University Press, 1905), p. 149.
11. Quoted by Laurie, S.S., *John Amos Comenius*, p. 55.
12. *The Great Didactic*, ch. ix.
13. *Ibid.*, ch. viii, 7.
14. *Ibid.*, ch. xxix, 2.
15. *The Great Didactic*, ch. xxiv, 2.
16. *Ibid.*, ch. xxi, 4.
17. *Ibid.*, ch. xix, 7, 8.
18. *Ibid.*, ch. xix, 14.
19. *Ibid.*, ch. xvi, 56 (ii).
20. *Ibid.*, ch. xvii, 17.
21. *Ibid.*, 42.
22. *Ibid.*, ch. xvii, 2 (viii), cf. 38 (iii).
23. *Ibid.*, ch. xviii, 28, cf. ch. xx.
24. *Ibid.*, ch. xvii, 27, 28.
25. *Ibid.*, ch. xxiv, 3-4.
26. *Ibid.*, ch. xii, 2.
27. *Ibid.*, ch. x, 1.
28. *Ibid.*, ch. xxx, 15. cf. ch. xix, 16-29.
29. *Ibid.*, ch. xvi, 7-10.
30. *Ibid.*, ch. xix, 14.
31. *The Great Didactic*, ch. xvi, 19.

32. *Ibid.,* ch. xvii, 13.
33. *Ibid.,* ch. xviii, 16.
34. Adams, J., *The Evolution of Educational Theory,* p. 267.
35. Boyd, W., *History of Western Education* (London : A & C Black, 1921), p. 263.
36. Spinka, *John Amos Comenius*, p. 146.
37. *Ibid.*, pp. 129-30.
38. Cf. Farrell, A.P., *The Jesuit Code of Liberal Education,* pp. 248-51.
39. *The Great Didactic*, ch. xix, 16.
40. *Ibid.*, ch. xvii, 41 (i).
41. Kandel I.L., in "National Education in an International World," *N.E.A. Journal* (April 1946), p. 175.

4

JEAN JACQUES ROUSSEAU

(1712-1778)

According to A. Hacker, "Aristotle believed in the wickedness of human nature, St. Augustine and St. Thomas affirmed the doctrine of original sin, and Machiavelli stated that men in general are, ungrateful, voluble, dissembler, anxious to avoid danger, and covetous of gain .... Rousseau has observed the men and the same perversities as have the theories which preceded him. The wicked behaviour of mankind has hardly escaped his eyes, yet this he says is a superficial view of man in society." According to Rousseau, man by birth had no evil tendencies. It was the result of wrong social actions which made him evil.

CONCEPT OF HUMAN NATURE

1. Self Love. Rousseau believed that man by nature has only two instincts, of them one is 'Self-love.' "His first preference always is to attend to his own presentation, his first cares are those which he owes himself."

2. Sympathy. Man's second instinct is that of sympathy or instinct of mutual aid. These instincts, Rousseau believed, always make our struggle for existence easier and do us more good than harm.

3. Conscience. There was every possibility of the clashing of both these instincts at one time or the other. As a result of clash another instinct called 'conscience' emerges. This conscience is something above education and reason. It resolves conflict between the first two instincts. Reasoning comes only when the complexities of problems come to the front. Sentiments attached with those instincts do not successfully motivate the actions of man in the proper direction.

4. Pride. A problem which is bound to crop is that if man was good by nature and gifted with the sentiments of love and sympathy then what makes the bad? Rousseau's simple answer was that self-love went astray to become 'pride' and the pride made man begin to feel ashamed or honoured over being deprived or getting something in competitions. This pride was the root cause of many evils. In his *Meaning of Rousseau*, Wright has said that "If we can give up pride, we can cease from all comparison with other men and simply go about our destiny. We can renounce a lot of imaginary desires and hold fast to the true things, needful casteway a world of illusion and disorder out of own self. We can be meek, and inherit our soul. In a word, we can return to nature. This is all the famous phrase means."

5. Freedom to choose. Rousseau also believed that in addition to above instincts Nature has also gifted us with another instinct namely the freedom to choose his own path which distinguished a man from an animal. This freedom was essential for the perfection of mankind.

STATE OF NATURE

1. Peaceful Ignorance. Rousseau believed that in the state of nature all lived an isolated life and had neither ties of obligation nor duties. Man did not know how to deliver a speech and had no cares for dress. He was free, self-contented and unknown to social good, evil or fear. He was not even afraid of death. He had no fear of loss of property or family because he had neither property nor family. Man was in peaceful ignorance. Rousseau ridiculed Hobbes by saying that "Above all, let us not conclude, with Hobbes, that because man has no idea of goodness, he does not know virtues; that he always refused to do his fellow creatures services which he does not think they have right to demand; or that by virtue of the right he truly claims everything he needs, he foolishly imagines himself the sole proprietor of the whole universe."

2. Group Life. Man could not lead a solitary life for long. His social instinct compelled him to live in groups. Social institutions began to develop gradually. Instinct of self-love began to shape itself into pride and man began to think in terms of having private property. The first man, having enclosed a piece of ground, he thought himself of saving, "This is mine and found other people simple enough to believe him, was the first real founder of civil society."

3. Property. Institution of private property, which entered the society, disturbed the whole atmosphere of pre-civil state. To quote Rousseau himself, "It came as a serpent and bit all. It brought misery, sorrow and evil in the minds of men who were otherwise good and noble." "So long as men remained content with their rustic huts ... and confined themselves to such arts as did not require several hands, they lived free, healthy, and happy lives so long as their nature allowed, as they continued to enjoy the pleasures of mutual and independent intercourse. But from the moment one man began to stand in need of the help of another; from the moment it appeared advantageous to any one to have provisions for two, equality disappeared, property was introduced; work became indispensable, and the vast forests became smiling fields; which man had to water with the sweat of his brows, and where slavery and misery were soon seen to germinate and grow up with the crops."

According to A. Hacker, "For a social system based on private property sets on egoistic standard for success, and it completes this standard in all individuals, men came to feel that they must own property, the superior to other man, in a world, be successful.... Not only men came to judge themselves as success or failures by social standard, they also became compulsive about the way they were viewed by those who lived around them."

The private property created a problem and the society was divided between the rich and poor. It also resulted in the division of labour. Thus, the whole set-up was disturbed. Rousseau said, "From these first distinctions arose on the one side vanity and contempt and on the other shame and envy; and the fermentation caused by these new heavens ended by producing combinations fatal to innocence and happiness." He concluded his discussion on the subject by saying that "In short, all men fall prey to frailties of their own age."

CONCEPT OF NEGATIVE EDUCATION

According to Rousseau, education means "Natural development of organs and powers of the child." The first education ought to be purely native. It consists not at all in teaching virtue or truth but in shielding the heart from vices and mind from errors. Thus, Rousseau was against imparting any education to the child. According to him, "In childhood the aim of education is not to utilise time but to lose it." Elsewhere he said, "A twelve-year old child should know nothing. The teacher should pay attention to the child only and not to knowledge."

CRITICISM OF CONTEMPORARY EDUCATION

In Rousseau's time the children were given moral and religious education through various books in order to prepare them for adult life. Explaining his new system of education Rousseau said, "Give me a twelve-year old child who does not know anything. By 15 years of age, I will teach him so much as other children read in 15 years of early life. The only difference will be that your student will be able to use it in practical life." Thus, Rousseau precisely reversed the old order. As he said, "Take the reverse of the accepted practices and you will always do right." This was what he called, negative education.

Criticising the educational system of his time Rousseau said, "That must we think them, of that barbarous education which sacrifices the present to an uncertain future, which loads a child with chains of every sort and begins by making him miserable in order to prepare for him long in advance, some pretended happiness which it is probable he will never enjoy." This was positive education emphasizing the mind and trying to make the child an adult. Negative education on the other hand, strengthens the sense organs and the power of reasoning. As Rousseau said, "Nature wants that the child should remain a child before he becomes an adult. By changing this sequence we shall get raw fruits which shall soon perish. The child has his own ways of seeing, thinking and experiencing. We should not impose our own ways of seeing, thinking and experiencing. We should not impose our own methods on him. It will be a folly." We do not understand the child and assume our ideas as his ideas. Elsewhere he said, "I want that some wise man should tell us the art of concealing the child. This art will be valuable for us. The teachers have not learnt even its elementary rule."

SELF-EDUCATION

Thus, negative education is self-education. It is the education of sense organs and body. This may be more possible in the play-ground rather than in the classroom. As Rousseau said, "We give too much importance to words. We produce by chattering education chatterers only. If you are all the time teaching morals to the child, then his mind will become useless. Whatever the child learns in playground is four times more useful than what he learns in the class." According to Rousseau, man's development may be classified into the following four stages :

1. *Infancy* : from birth to 5 years of age.
2. *Childhood* : from 5 years to 12 years of age.
3. *Adolescence* : from 12 years to 15 years of age.
4. *Youth* : from 15 years to 20 years of age.

Rousseau has suggested suitable education in all stages in his book *Emile*.

CURRICULUM OF EDUCATION

It is possible to arrive at Rousseau's concept of a curriculum from an analysis of the various stages of development, and it will be better to consider the curriculum in the same fashion.

1. Infancy. Rousseau was very critical of contemporary

curriculum laid down for the education of infants, because he stressed the fact that infants are not adults in the miniature. The child is not a young adult, because his instinct and tendencies are dissimilar to those of the adult. For this reason, it is imperative to first understand child psychology and then to frame a curriculum. Instead of giving him controlled information of various subjects at this stage, it is far more important to pay attention to the development of his body and his senses. Before thinking of making the child a successful engineer or doctor, it is desirable to make him healthy and self-sufficient young animal. In this age, the child can be taught a great deal through normal conversation carried on in the child's mother tongue. This will develop his linguistic ability. It is better not to try and still any kind of habits in the child at this stage. Rousseau stated, "The only habit the child should be allowed to contract is that of having no habits."

2. Childhood. Even in childhood, Rousseau objected to use of any textbook for education, because he wanted to keep Emile away from books of any kind upon the twelfth year. He thought it necessary to give the child a chance to learn everything through direct experience and observation. Education of this kind is based on the concept of negative education which suggests that the child mind should not be stuffed with information of different kinds. Instead he should be given liberty to learn through experience, because experience develops the sense organs which in turn lead to mental development, reason and development of the power of argument and reasoning. When the child is free to play, move, act at his own will during his childhood he goes through a variety of experiences and learns all kinds of activities. During childhood, the child should not be given any verbal lessons on history, geography or even language. It is not desirable even to do any moral preaching. Roosseau opined that the child will learn his morality by the natural consequences of his own actions. Hence, up to the childhood stage no curriculum of any kind is required.

3. Adolescence. Having arrived at the appropriate level of bodily and sensory development, the child can now be exposed to teaching according to a formal curriculum consisting of education in natural science, language, mathematics, woodwork, music, painting, social life and some kind of professional training. Even here, Rousseau opined, more stress should be laid on the use of the sense organs than books. The very object of training in all these various subjects is the training and development of the sense organs. The study of science will enhance the child's curiosity and his inclination towards research, invention and self-education. Painting helps to train the muscle and eyes. Handicrafts help in developing the ability to work, apart from the mental development which is part of the process. Passing through various phases of social life, the individual learns that men depend upon each other, and thereby the child learns to assume and fulfil social responsibility. Rousseau gave it as his opinion that books do not give knowledge, but only train one to talk. Hence, it is better if the curriculum for adolescence is based on active work than on books. During this period the adolescent must get adequate opportunity and time for hard work, education and study.

4. Youth. In the curriculum for youth, special stress has been laid on moral and religious education. But even moral education is to be derived through actual experience rather than through formal lectures. The youth learns a moral lesson when the sight of a physically handicapped person arouses in him the feeling of pity, sympathy and love. Religious education also follows the same pattern, but it can be assisted by the teaching of history, mythological stories and religious stories. The youth derives many lessons from these stories. Apart from moral and religious education, Rousseau gave appropriate immersions to education in bodily health, music and sex.

EDUCATIONAL METHOD

Rousseau is a naturalist in the methodology of education just as much as he is naturalist in the curriculum of education. He has stressed the importance of the two following principles governing the process of education.

1. Learning through Self-Experience. Rousseau wanted to educate Emile though experience and not through books. He was opposed to bookish education, because he contended that books try to teach one to talk about those things which one does not in fact know. That is why he wanted to keep Emile away from books for twelve years, so much so that he did not want Emile even to know what a book is. Rousseau has praised only one book, *Robinson Crusoe*, because it presents the natural needs of human beings in such a simple manner that the child can easily comprehend them. From this book the child can also learn the manner in which these needs are to be satisfied.

2. Learning through Doing. Rousseau opposed the rote method of learning on the ground that knowledge acquired through actual doing or actual experience is far more permanent than knowledge acquired through words. He wanted the child's power of reasoning and not his power of memorising things to be developed. That is why Rousseau was so severely critical of the existing methods of education. He wanted the child to become educated through his own observation, experience and analysis. Instead of stuffing the child's mind with his own knowledge the educator's task is to arouse the child's curiosity so that the child is inspired to find out things for himself, thus developing his own mind. Science is best taught through curiosity and the desire to experiment and research. Rousseau's insistence on these elements was later manifested in the evolution of the Heuristic method. If the child is to give moral education to himself he must be active. Long lectures bore the child, and instead of contributing to his education, only hinder it because they blunt the child's appetite for new things. Hence, instead of delivering long lectures to the child, it is better to give him the opportunity to act for himself. In education the object is more important than the word. It is undesirable to fashion a method of education and to mould the child accordingly.

DISCIPLINE

Rousseau, being a naturalist, wanted complete freedom as the first step towards inducing discipline in the child. He wanted a complete absence of any restraints on the child, because he felt that they hindered the development of discipline. It is better to leave the child free in free environment so that he can develop his natural powers. Rousseau's plan also did not include any arrangement for punishment, because he felt that punishment should be the natural outcome of his own mistakes. This is the naturalist conception of punishment. In this theory it is assumed that the child has no knowledge of good and bad, but he suffers pain when he makes a mistake and pleasure when work is properly done. This is the natural pattern of punishment, and it is the implied obedience of natural laws, because neglect or violation of these laws leads to pain and suffering. Hence, it is not necessary to lecture to the child. He is naturally possessed of a fine character, and this character is defiled by long lectures. He will learn better discipline, if he is left to himself.

SCHOOL ORGANISATION

The title given above may be a little misleading because Rousseau objected to the system of school education. He contended that the child is born innocent and pure, that he is only defiled and distorted by the defective environment of the school. In fact, the only suitable environment for the child is the natural one because the social environment of every kind is defective and impure. It is better to separate the child from his parents, to take him away from school, and leave him by himself in a natural environment. The educator's only task is to look after the child, because in natural surrounding the child will himself look after the development of his natural abilities. Even if schools are created, they can be utilised by stressing the natural surroundings instead of insisting on creating a social atmosphere. In the predominantly natural surroundings, the child will be able to develop naturally.

CONTRIBUTION OF ROUSSEAU'S NATURALISM TO EDUCATION

Like other systems of philosophy of education, naturalism has also made important contribution to education. It made education paedocentric, psychological, free, self-dependent, related to nature and society, based upon developmental psychology, democratic, multi-sided and natural to the stages of development. These points may now be discussed in detail.

1. Paedocentric Education. In the naturalistic conception of education, the child is in the forefront while all other things such as the educator, the books, the curriculum, the school, etc., are all in the background. Sir John Adams called this the conception of Paedocentric education. Naturalism stresses the fact that education should be guided by the nature of the child that the natural inclination of the child is completely good. Rousseau said, "Everything is good as it comes from the hands of the Author of Nature but everything degenerates in the hands of man." It is, therefore, argued that the child is naturally invested with all goodness, and all that is necessary is to protect him from a defective environment. He must be provided with the kind of environment which will encourage him to develop his innate goodness, his natural sense of the beautiful. He must be enabled to avoid the ugly, to manifest the natural truth inside him so that he can combat the falsity which is thrust upon him by the defective environment. In this process, the educator can perform only the function of the guide. Naturalists are not inclined to transform the child's nature through education or to apply to him the standards of the adult. Education, according to them, is not the preparation for life but life itself. Children should live like children, because infancy has its own significance, and it is not merely a stepping stone to adulthood. The child is not to be prepared and made ready for his future, but instead to be allowed to enjoy the present. Munro opines that Rousseau was the first to state the principle that, "Education finds its purposes, its process and its means wholly within the child life and the child experience." In this manner, it can be summarized that education is the process of living a natural life and moving towards evolution, because the child has within himself the germs of evolution.

2. Emphasis upon Psychology. The influence of naturalism was the cause of the psychological tendency gaining so much prominence in the field of education. By stressing the fact of the child's nature, it emphasised the importance of natural and what is abnormal in child development, the naturalists turned to be psychologists. Thus, it came to be understood that education must study the child and observe him. Many psychological researches have established that the child is not a young adult, that he has a distinct psychology which differs from adult psychology. It has been established that the child's mental activities of thinking, memory, imagination, recall, learning, etc., are different from similar activities in the adult. Hence, naturalism stressed the value of psychology for education.

3. Emphasis upon Free Choice. Naturalists contend that a predetermined pattern of education must never be foisted upon the child even when the pattern is entirely scientific. Education must give the child an opportunity of making a free choice in everything that he wants to study or play or even the manner in which he wants to behave. No external restraints should be placed on this free choice. Some naturalists even object to the very institution of school education, because they fear that the school is an obstacle in their normal independent development. They also believe that the atmosphere in the home is freer than the school environment but they are contradicted by others more conscious of the constant interruptions made by parents in the child's activities. Apart from this naturalists, in general, are opposed to all educands in one class being taught in the same manner, or by the same method of education. They even object to the introduction of any kind of timetable. One example of a completely unrestrained environment is to be found in Summerhill School established by A.S. Neil. It was taken for granted at this institution that the child was not expected to be fit for school, but that the school had to prepare itself for the child. Liberty was the first principle in the child's education, so much so that the children could play through the entire day if they were so inclined. They were given no religious education because a child is not naturally religiously inclined. No adult values were forced upon the children who were also taught none of the principles of culture. Naturalists also believe that the child should not be made cultured unless he realizes the need for culture. It was, therefore, better to leave the child in his more primitive condition. The liberty granted to the children even extended to their being allowed to roam naked if they so wished. It was found that no moral difficulty was raised due to the sex instinct, and it was decided that a healthy attitude to sex could only be generated through co-education. Neil was of the opinion that undesirable behaviour is due to moral and unnatural repression, and that no undesirable incidents take place due to co-education if the environment is completely free and liberal.

4. Role of the Teacher. Naturalism grants to the teacher the place of the friend and the guide, not of the administrator, for he is not to interfere in the child's activities, nor to make any attempt of influencing him. He is there merely to observe them, not to give them any information or to fill their minds with facts or to form their characters. It is for the child to decide what he wants to learn. He will know from experience what he should learn and when, what he should do and what he should avoid. His interests should be given an opportunity to manifest themselves freely. All this does not imply that the teacher has no role at all in education, for he has definite role in as much as he is the one who will provide the educative material, create the opportunities for learning, create the ideal environment and thus contribute to the child's development. For example, in the Montessori method of education, the child is given many kinds of equipment to play with, while the teacher looks on and observes. Naturalism, thus, favours the concept of self-education. Norman Mancken has gone one step further and suggested that children can even educate each other. Nothing should be done with a view to turning the child's mind in any particular direction. He is not to be taught to read or write, to make use of the various parts of his body, or be taught moral lessons, but merely to be left to himself so that he can develop independently. This is what Rousseau implied by his concept of the educator's negative effort in the process of education. Negative effort did not imply that the teacher was merely to pass his time, but to observe the child, avoid any interference in his activities, to prevent or protect him from defects, to protect him from a defective environment. The educator must be perfectly aware of all that he has not to do, but at the same time this negative attitude is to be supplemented by the positive one of love and sympathy. He can love the child only when he himself has been a child, that is, he has not completely forgotten his childhood. He should have the inclination to laugh and play like the child, to forget that he is an adult, to mix with the children and become one of them himself. Only then can he give anything to them.

At times, one finds children developing some bad tendencies and it becomes necessary to guide them. But even this should be done in the form of an informal conversation with the child. In such a dialogue the educator understands the difficulties of the educated, shows his love and sympathy and encourages the educand to solve them himself. He makes the educand aware of the difficulties he is likely to face. Neil called this re-education. He saw in his own school that many of the children often sought opportunities for such informal dialogue. Whenever the children showed any disinclination for such dialogues, they were immediately abandoned.

5. Emphasis on Direct Experience. Naturalists believe Rousseau's dictum, "Give your scholar no verbal lessons; he should be taught by experience alone." Hence, the naturalist lays stress on teaching through direct experience. The child will learn more by coming into contact through the objects surrounding him than through books. He should be allowed to examine these objects. Similarly, the teaching of science should not take the form of verbal lectures, but actual performance of experiments in the laboratory. Geometry should be taught not by the problems written in books but by actual measurement of the areas of the school and the height and other dimensions of the school buildings and other objects. If geography is to be taught, the educand should be taken to the various parts of the country, and not taught only through maps and charts produced on the blackboard. Thus, naturalists insists that the educand must learn from the things that exist in the school, not through the lectures of the educator.

6. Emphasis on Direct Experience of Social Life. What is true of the natural environment of the child, is also equally true of the social environment in which he lives. He should learn the various duties, obligations and responsibilities of social life not through lectures of the educator but through the natural society of the school, of which the educand is a member. Here, left to himself, he will learn to do those things which should be done and leave alone those which should be avoided. In Neil's Summerhill School the children themselves decided upon the form of behaviour which others found objectionable or which hindered their adjustment, and thus learnt to avoid it. This formed the basis of the child's social education. The concept of co-education is also favoured by the naturalists because the society within the school resembles more closely the society outside school. Besides, it has been contended that unnatural attitudes to sex are the inevitable result of segregated education of boys and girls. This is a very controversial subject and many educationalists fail to agree with the naturalists, although in many cases the results of experiments in co-education favoured the naturalists' thesis. It can undoubtedly be said, however, that the child's experience of the social life within the school, forms the basis of his later social and moral life.

7. Self-Government. Another characteristic feature of the naturalist conception of education is the insistence on self-government. Neil's Summerhill School experimented in this direction also by allowing the educands to form their own government. They created a cabinet of five educands whose function it was to reflect on various difficulties, to give decisions in cases of indiscipline and even to inflict punishment for such acts. These five cabinet members met every Saturday night, and one of them was elected to the chair. All problems were then discussed. The cabinet even had the authority to expel an educand from the school, if it so decided, although, in fact, this right was never exercised. Neil states that this arrangement of self-government is very beneficial for training educands in democratic living. The condition of self-government does not impose certain restrictions on the educand's activities, but because it is imposed through his own rules and regulations, it takes the form of self-government and self-discipline. All kinds of self-control, can be learnt through self-government, and it has some of the drawbacks of the method of external control. There is, undoubtedly, no better way of teaching public morality. And it is only self-government which teaches cultured behaviour and co-operation.

8. Play-way of Education. Of the many methods of education, naturalists prefer the play-way. In this technique, all that the child learns is through a feeling of playing or indulging in sport. Psychologists contend that the child best manifests his instincts and tendencies in an independent game and his development can also be achieved through sport. Whatever the objectives of play, the recapitualation of man's primitive activities, the preparation for future life, or a kind of safety value for an individual's excessive energy — it is, undoubtedly, the most natural method of teaching. Playing affords education not only during childhood, for people learn many things through playing even in adult life. Games are an important medium of constructive or creative education. Nuturalists have, therefore, placed adequate stress on the value of games, a fact which even modern educationalists accept without reservation. Now-a-days the play-way of education is adopted for the education of infant and children and thus they acquire all the advantages of a naturalist's education. Montessori education, for example, is a good instance of this because in this method of teaching, the child learns even reading and writing through play. Scouting is another activity in which the child is taught many things through play. In Neil's Summerhill School, more stress was placed on character than on learning. Children were free to play from morning till evening. There was no system of examination and books had less importance in the school than most other kinds of activities. Some lessons were taught, but attendance was never compulsory because most of the work, in any case, was done outside the classroom. On the other hand, educands favoured the crafts rooms much more where they were taught to make things out of wood, plastic and metal. Educands and educators sat together to write plays. It was found that drama writing is an important means of developing the creative imagination.

9. Natural Development of the Child. Naturalists stressed the fact that the child must develop according to his own nature and educational pattern must be modified to suit the various needs of children, because children differ from each other on account of their innate individual differences.

10. Value of Developmental Psychology. By stressing the value of studying child development, naturalists made contributions to the progress of developmental psychology which scientifically studies the various stages of man's development.

11. Comprehensive Curriculum. Naturalists have favoured the adoption of a multifaced and comprehensive curriculum, which reflects, apart from the scientific, sociological and psychological tendencies, the holistic tendency in education. The holistic approach is, in fact, a synthesis of the scientific, sociological and psychological tendencies. Schools make use of all kinds of modern audio-visual aids, and arrange for teaching of science and the various arts. Extra-curricular programmes and activities are also believed to be of considerable importance.

12. Development of Democratic Traits. Naturalism is opposed to repression and vigorous discipline of any kind. It seeks to replace the traditional by the modern, the dogmatic by the liberal and the progressives. It consequently helps in the development of such democratic qualities as liberty, equality and fraternity. It favours a complete rejection of the additional modes of teaching and instead advocates greater dependence upon self-government.

13. Development of Child Psychology. Naturalists played a significant role in the development of child psychology as a result of their insistence on education being oriented to the child's nature. As a result of this development in child psychology, it was discovered that the child is not a young adult, but a distinct kind of human being possessed of different psychology. Naturalists insist that the child is born good, and that education must seek only to protect him from evil.

14. Support to Residential Schools. Under the naturalist mode of teaching, the educator has a negative role of protecting the educand from evil. For this reason naturalists favour residential schools because the educand's environment can be controlled much better if the educand lives in hostels attached to the school. They also favour the pattern of co-education because this develops moral natural attitude in boys and girls.

15. Revolution in All Fields of Education. Finally, it can be said that naturalists were responsible for some of most revolutionary ideas in all spheres of education. As has already been pointed out, naturalists vigorously opposed all traditional thinking on child psychology, education techniques, curriculum, administration, co-education, etc. Although all their ideas are not found acceptable today, many of the principles propounded by the naturalists are still being applied. For example, such educational principles as learning through activity, going from the simple to the complex, from the concrete to the abstract, from the definite to the indefinite, from the easy to the difficult, and from the known to the unknown, are all principles which were originally propounded by the naturalists. And all these have been established as correct. Modern educationists now agree that the aim of education is not to provide education but to encourage spontaneous development. The significance and efficacy of broad-based and comprehensive curricula have been almost universally accepted. Frustration and repression are held to be harmful everywhere. And the role of the teacher is now universally seen as the guide and not administrator.

5

PESTALOZZI
(1746-1827)

Among the great educators Pestalozzi appears a man afflicted with new ideas which he found himself unable to formulate or to put effectively into practice. In his *Swansong* (1826) he admitted,[1] "My Lofty ideals were preeminently the product of a kind, well meaning soul, inadequately endowed with the intellectual and practical capacity which might have helped considerably to further my heartfelt desire. It was the product of an extremely vivid imagination which in the stress of my daily life proved unable to produce any important results."[2] Pestalozzi arrived at his principles mostly by intuition. In one work he described his educational ideal in the form of a romance. In another, he is metamorphosed into a pedantic drill-master in arithmetic pleased with himself for having filled a thick book with the multiplication table. However, his reputation attracted philosophers like Fitche and Herbart who not only critically examined his system but also published their versions of it. In fact, no great European educator has ever had such a succession of distinguished visitors to his schools.

EDUCATIONAL AIM IN LIFE

Pestalozzi's aim in life was to ameliorate the lot of the poor. As Herbart commented, "The welfare of the people is Pestalozzi's aim.... He did not seek the wreath of merit in your mansions but in their hovels."[3] "His humanitarianism was reinforced by his reading of Rousseau's works in early youth. This aim compelled him to concentrate on the fundamentals of education, for, as Herbart remarks, "the most pressing needs are the more universal." Pestalozzi was thus forced to formulate a practical scheme of education suitable for all, and to lay the foundation of an elementary school system. In the *Letters to Greaves* he stated, "It (the end held out as the highest object of all man's efforts) must embrace all mankind; it must be applicable to al!, without distinction of zones, or nations in which they may be born. It must acknowledge the rights of man in the fullest sense of the word.... They embrace the rightful claims of all classes to a general diffusion of useful knowledge, a careful development of the intellect, and judicious attention to all the faculties of man — physical, intellectual and moral."[4]

Echoing Rousseau's dictum "Life is the trade I would teach him,"[5] Pestalozzi maintained that the ultimate end of education is not a perfection in the accomplishments of the school but fitness for life.[6] In *How Gertrude Teaches Her Children* he elaborated, "We have spelling schools, writing schools, catechism schools, and we want — men's schools."[7]

Pestalozzi settled at Neuhof in 1774 and introduced a number of beggar children and waifs into his house to rescue them from their degraded condition, hoping to restore their self-respect and manhood — to educate the poor for poverty — but the scheme failed and the institution was closed in 1779. In his *Ansichten and Erfahrungen*[8] he explained that he not only tried to find work for the poor children, but also wished to warm their hearts and to develop their minds, and through self instruction to elevate them to a sense of the inner dignity and worth of their nature. He also acknowledged his failure, admitting that he took upon his own shoulders a burden which he could not bear and which he should have left to others, and thereby exhausted himself, plunged himself into domestic confusion and brought indescribable suffering on himself.

After the failure at Neuhof, a literary interlude ensued. Pestalozzi works, *Evening Hours of* a *Hermit* and *Leonard and Gertrude : A Book for the People*, both appeared in 1780. The former was to serve as a preface to all that Pestalozzi should write in the future. In it he warned parents not to hurry their children into working at things remote from their immediate interests, and after the manner of Rousseau, not to anticipate the ordinary course of their development. The danger lies in children's lessons dealing with words before they have actually encountered the real things. Hermann Krusi, one of Pestalozzi's coadjutors, in *My Educational Recollections*, writes how before his meeting with Pestalozzi at Burgdorf he held the system in high estimation which could elicit answers from the children by dexterous questions. He continues, "Having read in educational writings that Socrates had possessed this faculty in a high degree, the term, 'to Socratize' presented to me an almost magic charm. When I communicated my views on this subject to Pestalozzi he could not refrain from a knowing smile. 'This art,' he then said quite earnestly, when applied at the proper time and place, has its own value, but it is utterly worthless for teachers and children in the public schools. Socrates was surrounded by young men who had a background in the knowledge of words and things. If you take pains to give your children first this background, then the necessary questions about things within their own observation will be naturally suggested. Without this background every attempt to elicit proper answers from the children by artfully put questions is merely thrashing of straw, and leads to sore deception or discouragement which may even deprive you of faith in yourself."

Leonard and Gertrude described how, mainly by means of education, the regeneration of a small community was affected by the noble efforts of a pious woman, the wife of a village mason in humble circumstances. In the village of Bonnal, the home of Leonard becomes the model educational institution, and Gertrude, the mother of the children, the ideal educator. This home-education represents Pestalozzi's ideal. It was only the circumstances in which he laboured that compelled him in practice to adopt class-teaching methods. These he regarded as a necessary but temporary expedient till mothers in sufficient numbers should be adequately educated to superintend the instruction of their own children.

As yet there was no formal analysis but the 'contact with realities' for which Pestalozzi pleaded in his *Evening Hours of a Hermit* is exemplified in the procedure of Gertrude. Yet she never adopted the tone of instructor toward her children; she did not say to them, 'Child, this is your head, your nose, your hand, your finger;' or 'Where is your eye, your ear?' but instead she would say : 'Come here, child, I will wash your little hands,' 'I will comb your hair,' or 'I will cut your fingernails.' Her verbal instruction seemed to vanish in the spirit of her real activity, in which it always had its source. The result of her system was that each child was skilful, intelligent, and active to the full extent that his age and development allowed.

"The instruction she gave them in the rudiments of arithmetic was intimately connected with the realities of life. She taught them to count the number of steps from one end of the room to the other, and two of the rows of five panes each, in one of the windows, gave her an opportunity to unfold the decimal relations of numbers. She also made them count their threads while spinning, and the number of turns on the reel, when they wound the yarn into skeins. Above all, in every occupation of life she taught them an accurate and intelligent observation of common objects and the forces of nature."

ANOTHER EXPERIMENT

Between December 1798 and June 1799 another opportunity presented itself to Pestalozzi to put his ideas into practice, this time at Stanz. About eighty children, left destitute after the village had been reduced to ashes by the French troops, were put in Pestalozzi's charge. But the population being Catholic were naturally hostile to the representative of a government which had brought ruin upon them. The retreating French forces commandeered the convent where Pestalozzi was established, and ended the experiment. Nevertheless some measure of success attended his efforts. It illustrated the truth of his view that education should be based on love. The great human sympathy for children with which Pestalozzi was endowed in a singular degree had prevailed. But affection, even when it is reciprocal, is not enough. The pupil must be trained to independence. As Herbart insists, "Something more than a love for a subject is required of the youth; a well-balanced, many-sided interest is demanded."[9]

VENTURE AT BURGDORF

Pestalozzi's next venture was at Burgdorf (1799-1804). It was here that he developed and formulated his teaching technique. The Burgdorf period produced Pestalozzi's most important treatise on educational method, *How Gertrude Teaches Her Children or Letters to Gessner* (1801). Reviewing this work, Herbart states, "It is his intention to place in the hand of wholly ignorant teachers and parents such writings as they need only to cause the children to read off and learn by heart, without adding anything of their own. What he believed could be carried into effect most immediately he preferred; he must have his levers sturdy enough not to break even in clumsy hands. The book in which, under the form of letters to a friend, he describes the outlines of such a plan, belongs really in the hands of such men as have influence on the organisation of the lowest schools and upon parents of the lowest social ranks. Such men would be able to spread his actual school books, which are to be published in the future. What is faulty in the whole publication therefore, is, perhaps, its title, which brings it immediately into the hands of women, of mothers."[10]

Pestalozzi's intention, as he himself conceived it,[11] was to discover the nature of teaching itself, to found popular instruction on psychological principles, to produce a general method of instruction following a psychologically ordered sequence.

Although the title and the form of Pestalozzi's chief work mentioned above were unfortunate, it was nevertheless the main source of his contributions to the psychology, sociology and philosophy of education. Of the Pestalozzian method Herbart says, "Its peculiar merit consists in having laid hold more boldly and more zealously than any former method of the duty of building up the child's mind, of constructing in it a definite experience in the light of clear sense-perception, not acting as if the child had already an experience but taking care that he gets one.... The Pestalozzian method, therefore, is by no means qualified to crowd out any other method but to prepare the way for it. It takes care of the earliest age that is capable of receiving instruction."[12]

CONCEPT OF *ANSCHAUUNG*

Herbart here refers to Pestalozzi's conception of *Anschauung*, a term for which there is no precise English equivalent. By *Anschauung* is to be understood the immediate experience of objects or situations. Terms used by English and American writers to convey the same idea include : immediate awareness, direct acquaintance, direct appreciation, concrete experience, personal contact, first-hand impressions, face-to-face knowledge, the direct impact of things and persons.

Anschauung is the basis of all knowledge and experience. It is not, however, restricted to mere awareness of objects. It comprises also spontaneous appreciation of moral actions and direct realisation of situations. It emphasises the immediacy of the experience, but does not imply simplicity in the process. Negatively it excludes the intervention of any object or process between the subject and his experiences. Its primary purpose, for Pestalozzi, was to further the converse of man with his world.

For Kant the forms of *Anshauung* were space and time. In his *Letters to Greaves* Pestalozzi accepts Kant's classification, "The relations and proportions of number and form constitute the natural measure of all those impressions which the mind receives from without. They are the measures, and comprehend the qualities of the number the measure of time." Earlier, and generally, he distinguished three aspects of *Anshauung*, namely, form, number and name. How he arrived at this division he recorded as follows,[13] "Living, but vague, ideas of the elements of instruction whirled about in my mind for a long time.... At last, like a *Deus ex machina*, came the thought — the means of making clear all knowledge gained by sense-impression comes from number, form and language. It suddenly seemed to throw a new light on what I was trying to do.

"Now, after my long struggle, or rather my wandering reverie, I aimed wholly and simply at finding out how a cultivated man behaves, and must behave, when he wishes to distinguish any object which appears misty and confused to his eyes, and gradually to make it clear to himself."

Threefold Observation

In this case he will observe three things :

1. How many, and what kinds of objects are before him.
2. Their appearance, form or outline.
3. Their names; how he may represent each of them by a sound or word.

Threefold Powers

The result of this action in such a man manifestly presupposes the following ready-formed powers :

1. The power of recognising unlike objects, according to the outline, and of representing to oneself what is contained within it.
2. That of stating the number of these objects, and representing them to himself as one or many.
3. That of representing objects, their number and form, by speech, and making them unforgettable.

Threefold Principle

It also thought number, form and language are, together, the elementary means of instruction, because the whole sum of the external properties of any object is comprised in its outline and its number, and is brought home to by consciousness through language. It must then be an immutable law of the technique of instruction to start from and work within this threefold principle :

1. To teach children to look upon every object that is brought before them as a unit, that is, as separated from those with which it is connected.

2. To teach them the form of every object, that is, its size and proportions.
3. As soon as possible to make them acquainted with all the words and names descriptive of objects known to them.

Cultivation of Primary Faculties

And as the instruction of children should proceed from these three elementary points, it is evident that the first effort of the technique of instruction should be directed to the primary faculties of counting, measuring, and speaking, which lie at the basis of all accurate knowledge of objects of sense. We should cultivate them with strictest psychological technique of instruction, endeavour to strengthen and make them strong, and to bring them, as a means of development and culture, to the highest pitch of simplicity, consistency and harmony.

Apprehension of form was developed by Pestalozzi mainly through drawing, on the ground that children are ready at an earlier age for knowledge of proportion and for the guidance of the slate-pencil than for guiding the pen and making tiny letters.

Pestalozzi built all power of doing, even the power of clear representation of all real objects, upon the early development of the ability to draw lines, angles, rectangles and curves. Thus he states that "By exercises in lines, angles and curves, a readiness in gaining sense-impressions of all kinds is produced in the children, as well as skill of hand, of which the effect will be to make everything that comes within the sphere of their observation gradually clear and plain." Against the tendency for the means to obscure the aim, and for drawing to become an and in itself, Pestalozzi protested, saying "Nature gives the child no lines, she only gives him things, and lines must be given him only in order that he may perceive things rightly. The things must not be taken from him in order that he may see only lines."[14] And concerning the danger of rejecting Nature for the sake of lines, on another occasion he angrily exclaimed, "God forbid that I should overwhelm the human mind and harden it against natural sense-impressions, for the sake of these lines and of the technique of instruction, as idolatrous priests have overwhelmed it with superstitious teaching, and hardened it against natural sense-impressions."[15]

TEACHING WRITING

By basing writing on drawing, separating the acquisition of the forms from the command of the writing instrument, and using the skill acquired in writing for the expression of significant ideas, Pestalozzi anticipated in many points the Montessori method of teaching writing. The defect of his method, as in language teaching, is that he carried his analysis to its ultimate limits. What is psychologically simple to the child is not necessarily what remains when analysis cannot be carried further. In writing, the unit is the word or the letter, not the so-called element of the letter.

TEACHING OF ARITHMETIC

Scope for the application of Pestalozzi's principle of concreteness was readily found in arithmetic. Reviewing Krusi's development as a teacher, Pestalozzi wrote, "For instance, when he asked in arithmetic, 'How many times is seven contained in sixty-three?' the child had no real background for his answer, and must with great trouble dig it out of his memory. How, by the plan of putting nine times seven objects before his eyes, and letting him count them as nine sevens standing together, he has not to think any more about this question; he knows from what he has already learnt, although he is asked for the first time, that seven is contained nine times in sixty-three. So it is in other department of the method."[16] The general principle of *Anshauung* as applied to arithmetic Pestalozzi formulated in these terms, "That by exercising children beginning to count with real objects, or at least with dots representing them, we lay the foundation of the whole of the science of arithmetic, and secure their future progress from error and confusion."[17]

LANGUAGE TEACHING

With the language aspect of *Anshauung* Pestalozzi concerned himself more particularly, although he did not quite regard the name as coordinate in rank with form and number.[18] Fichte complains,[19] that acquaintance with the word-sign adds nothing to the knowledge of an object but simply brings it within the sphere of what can be communicated to others. Herbart nevertheless comes again to the defence of Pestalozzi arguing[20] that to young children a word, a name, is not as to us merely the sign of a thing. The word itself is the thing. They linger upon the sound. Not until the latter has become commonplace to them do they learn to forget it in attention to the thing itself. Pestalozzi reasoned that the child must learn to talk before he can be taught to read, and recognised the child's for a full and facile vocabulary. Thus, he affirmed, "The advantage of a fluent and early nomenclature is invaluable to children. The firm impression of names makes the things unforgettable, as soon as they are brought to their knowledge; and the stringing together of names in an order based upon reality and truth develops and maintains in them a consciousness of the real relation of things to each other. Certain it is that when a child has made the greater part of a scientific nomenclature his own, he enjoys through it at least the advantage that a child enjoys who in his own, a great house of business, daily becomes acquainted from his cradle upwards with the names of countless objects."[21] Pestalozzi does not propose that the child should acquire a stock of names merely for their own sake but as a means to the mastery of things, a function which the name has had from the earliest times. He complained[22] that in the lower schools for more than a century there had been given to empty words a weight in the human mind that not only hindered attention to the impressions of nature, but even destroyed man's inner susceptibility to these expressions. His own method, he explained, was "like Nature with the savage, I always put the picture before the eye, and then sought for a word, for the picture."[23]

Pestalozzi reduced language to words or names, and the latter he resolved into sounds. For each stage he constructed formal exercises, beginning with syllables which he regarded as the irreducible elements. The first exercises took the form, for example, a – ab – bab, etc., much after the manner of the present-day phonic method of teaching to read. Lists of names of the most important objects in all divisions of the kingdom of nature, history, geography, human callings and relations he required to be memorised, and lastly sentences had to be formed in various ways. Pestalozzi's analysis was carried to extremes and evoked censure. The redeeming feature of his method was nevertheless that it based reading on sounds and not on spelling, and thereby prepared the way for modern methods. In *The Mother's Book*, Pestalozzi was led into beginning with the child's body, arguing that the first object of the child's knowledge must be the child himself.

Immediate experience is generally confused and must be made definite; it must likewise be generalised. In his *Letters to Greaves* Pestalozzi explains, "But if a mother is to teach by THINGS, she must recollect also that to the formation of an idea more is requisite than bringing the object before the senses. Its qualities must be explained; its origin must be accounted for; its parts must be described, and their relation to the whole ascertained; its use, its effects or consequences must be stated. All this must be done, at least, in a manner sufficiently clear and comprehensive to enable the child to distinguish the object from other objects, and to account for the distinction which is made."[24]

NO GAPS IN INSTRUCTION

In this progressive development no step must be missed. There must be no gaps in instruction. This is Pestalozzi's principle of unbroken sequence or uninterrupted continuity, second in significance only to his doctrine of *Anschauung*. It was the feature of his teaching that appealed to and was championed by Herbart.

PRACTICAL AIM OF EDUCATION

Although *How Gertrude Teaches Her Children* is mainly concerned with the nature and development of knowledge, Pestalozzi would not have it thought that this is the aim of education, for he says, "To have knowledge without practical power, to have insight, and yet to be incapable of applying it in everyday life, what more dreadful fate could an unfriendly spirit devise for us?"[25]

THE EDUCATIONAL PROCESS

Of the threefold division of the educational process — the physical, the intellectual, the moral, religious — the first comprises not merely physical culture but also artistic skill and technical dexterity since all involve the physical organs. Fichte approved of the inclusion by Pestalozzi of the development of the pupil's bodily powers, quoting a passage from *How Gertrude Teaches Her Children*. But, he complained that Pestalozzi has failed to supply a graduated scheme of physical exercise.

VIEW ABOUT ART

While mental development in general consists in the inner organisation of impressions received from without, art reverses the process in so far as it modifies the external world by means of inner impulses and tendencies. The basis of all art is partly internal, partly external; partly mental, partly physical. Artistic skill comprises the effort to embody the products of the human mind, to give expression to the impulses of the human heart, to exercise the dexterities required in domestic and social life. Such is Pestalozzi's view of art as expounded in *The Swansong*. The development of dexterity follows the same laws as the development of knowledge.

MORAL EDUCATION

Following Rousseau Pestalozzi believed that the child is born good. But we must nevertheless take his education out of the hands of blind nature, as the world he entered is a world spoilt alike for the innocent enjoyment of the senses and for the feelings of his inner nature.[26] The moral faculty is present in infancy. "God has given the child a spiritual nature, that is to say, He has implanted in him the voice of conscience; and He has done more, He has given him the faculty of attending to this voice."[27] The moral virtues originate in the relations existing between the child and his mother. In them too lies the whole essence of the natural germ of that state of mind which is peculiar to human dependence on the Author of our being.

EQUALITY OF DIVISIONS

In his earlier writings Pestalozzi stressed the equality rather than the correlation of his three main divisions of education — the physical, the intellectual and the ethico-religious, or — the physical, the technical, the aesthetic, the intellectual, the moral and the religious aspects of personality. In his later writings he insisted that three aspects should be coordinated by one spiritual principle. Thus, in The *Swansong* he definitely characterised the relationship between them as one of harmony. "The education of all three sides of our nature proceeds on common lines in equal measure, as is necessary if the unity of our nature and the equilibrium of our powers are to be recognised from the outset."[28] And in the *Letters of Greaves* he states that "The powers of man must be so cultivated that no one shall predominate at the expense of another, but each be excited to the true standard of activity; and this standard is the spiritual nature of man."[29]

Earlier the idea of harmonious development was mentioned in *How Gertrude Teaches Her Children*. "The aim of all instruction is, and can be, nothing but the development of human nature, by the harmonious cultivation of its powers and talents, and the promotion of manliness of life." Emphasis on harmonious development or on well-balanced training, should not blind us to the fact that education should respect individuality. In *The Swansong* Pestalozzi advises, "Unusual capacity should be given possible chance, and, above all, it should be rightly guided."

In 1805 Pestalozzi was transferred from Burgdorf to Yverdon, where he remained till 1827. He had by now acquired international fame. Princes visited his institution. "The powerful, indefinable, string and uplifting effect produced by Pestalozzi when he spoke, set one's soul on fire for a higher, nobler life," writes Froebel, "although he had not made clear or sure the exact way towards it, nor indicated the means whereby to attain it. Thus did the power and many-sidedness of the educational effort make up for the deficiency in unit and comprehensiveness; and the love, the warmth, the stir of the whole, the human kindness and benevolence of it replaced the want of clearness, depth, thoroughness, extent, perseverance and steadiness."[30]

Pestalozzi's efforts in education were tentative. Although lacking the scientific precision demanded today, they were experimental. His results had not that consistency which obtains in a purely apriori scheme of education, nor did they command that respect which attaches to the conclusion of a philosophical theory. As the products of hard won experience they nevertheless possess a reliability which many other more pretentious systems do not. To conclude in the words of Robert R. Rusk, "With Pestalozzi it may truly be said that necessity was the mother of invention. It was this necessity that constrained him to make *Anschuung* the common starting-point of all instruction, to insist that teaching should follow an orderly sequence, to formulate a general method based on psychological principles, to recognise the practical and emotional aspects of personality, to lay the basis of our elementary school system and to reinforce the democratic traditions in education."[31]

REFRENCES

1. *Pestalozzi's Educational Writings*, edited by J.A. Green (London : Edward Arnold, 1912), p. 228.
2. Herbart, *Minor Pedagogical Works*, pp. 36-37.
3. *Ibid.*, p. 36.
4. *Letters on Early Education* (1827), p. 80.
5. *Emile*, p. 9.
6. *Letters to Greaves*, p. 85.
7. *How Gertrude Teaches Her Children*, by J.H. Pestalozzi, translated by Lucy E. Holland and Francis C. Turner (London : Swan Sonnenschein & Co., 1907), p. 178.
8. *Ansichten and Effahrungen* (1807).
9. *Minor Pedagogical Works*, pp. 74-76.

10. *Minor Pedagogical Works*, pp. 37-38.
11. *Ibid.*, pp. 19, 25, 139.
12. *Minor Pedagogical Works*, p. 61.
13. Pestalozzi, J.H., *How Gertrude Teaches Her Children,* pp. 86-88; cf. pp. 33, 51-52.
14. *Ibid.*, p. 69.
15. *Ibid.*
16. *Ibid.*, p. 54.
17. *Ibid.*, p. 51.
18. *Ibid.*
19. *Addresses to the German Nation*, English translation, p. 166.
20. *Minor Pedagogical Writings,* p. 38.
21. *Ibid.*, p. 33.
22. *Ibid.*, p. 113.
23. *Ibid.*, p. 55.
24. *Ibid.*, p. 123.
25. *Ibid.*, p. 173.
26. *Ibid.*, p. 187.
27. *Letters to Greaves*, p. 19.
28. Green, J.A. *Pestalozzi's Educational Writings*, p. 281.
29. *Op. cit.*, p. 18.
30. *Ibid.*, pp. 156-57.
31. Rusk, Robert R., *The Doctrines of Great Educators* (London : Macmillan, 1954), p. 208.

6

FREIDRICH FROEBEL

(1782-1852)

PHILOSOPHICAL BACKGROUND

By reason of his irregular training, Froebel neither adopted nor developed a consistent philosophic attitude. As he himself explains in a letter to Krause, he stated, "Without ceasing to systematise, symbolise, idealise, realise and recognise, identities and analogies amongst all facts and all problems, expressions, and formulae; and in this way, life with all varied phenomena and activities became more and more free from contradictions, more harmonious, simple and clear, and more recognisable as a part of the life universal."[1]

Philosophy of Kant set himself to determine the conditions of knowledge or of experience. He found that it was impossible to account for experience as a mere reflection of nature. Hume had tried this and ended in scepticism. The other alternative was that nature must conform to our method of conceiving it. The world of science was found to be arranged in space and time. Its phenomena were connected in a causal series. According to Kant, this arrangement and determination resulted from the fact that the mind is so constituted that only thus is experience possible for it. The world apprehended by the forms of space and time and conceived in accordance with the categories of substance, cause, etc., is the phenomenal world. Kant leaves open the possibility of another form of experience by postulating the existence of the noumenal world which cannot be known through perception and understanding, but which might be experienced by an intuitive intelligence.

When we attempt to apply the forms of perception and the categories of the understanding beyond the sphere of the phenomenal world, such application gives rise to antinomies or conflicting conclusions. For example, it can be proved that the world had a beginning and that it had no beginning; that it had a First Cause and that it had no First Cause; that the soul is a simple substance and that it is not so. From the antinomies Kant draws the conclusion that the conclusions of cause, substance, etc., are valid only within the phenomenal sphere. It is their application beyond this sphere that creates the antinomies.

In his *Critique of Pure Reason,* Kant restricted the application of the conceptions of space, time, substance, cause, etc., to the scientific realm, reserving the possibility of the existence of another realm where freedom would be possible, and the immortality of the soul and the existence of God would not be self-contradictory conceptions. Opposed to the phenomenal world he set the noumenal world, regarded as mere limiting conception implying the possibility of a form of experience other than the material and scientific.

In the *Critique of Practical Reason,* Kant maintained that the noumena have positive significance and content. In the ethical sphere the conception of duty is a positive conception which in its mature demands freedom. Thus, for Kant there were two spheres in which man lived the phenomenal or scientific world governed by the conception of cause, and the noumenal or ethical world characterised by freedom. Kant failed to relate these two spheres satisfactorily to each other. But to him is due the credit of demonstrating that either alone is incomplete. He made both materialism and naturalism untenable. By establishing the priority of the ethical life and the reality of the spiritual realm Kant laid the foundation of modern idealism.

The Educational Corollary of Kant's Doctrine

In opposition to, but not incompatible with, a mechanical concatenation of external phenomena stands a free inner synthetic or creative activity. The priority assigned by Kant to the inner and determining aspect of experience gave the necessary philosophical support to the psychological treatment of education which was characteristic of succeeding educational thought.

The task of the successors of Kant was to resolve the dualism inherent in his system. His naturalistic and realistic interpreters, insisted on the connectedness and completeness of the phenomenal world, and resolved the realities of the noumenal or intelligible world — God, freedom and immortality — into mere serviceable illusions. On the other hand, Fichte, emphasised the noumenal character of intelligible world to such an extent as to reduce the phenomenal world to a mere appearance or illusion. The free activity of reason or self-consciousness could not be conditioned by anything alien to itself. Fichte consequently assumed that the object which consciousness demanded as a necessary condition of its own existence and progressive realisation was not a mere sensuous element externally 'given,' but a product of the self-estranging process of consciousness itself.

Schelling's Standpoint

Schelling's standpoint was, at the outset, practically identical with that of Fichte. However, in his later writings he sought to correct the overstatement of Fichte which tended to reduce nature to a nonentity, by insisting that the Absolute equally manifests itself in nature and in spirit, and that the intelligence could find itself in nature as well as in itself.

Influenced by Schelling

In his *Autobiography* Froebel admitted that he was acquainted with Schelling's work *On the World Soul*, stating "What I read in that book moved me profoundly, and I thought I understood it."[2] In his work Schelling "seeks mainly for a principle which shall reduce the whole of nature to unity. This principle must not be sought in any transcendental, supernatural region, whether called God or Fate, but in nature itself. A principle such as is sought, Schelling seemed to find in a conception of matter as a unity of opposite forces, and hence he naturally attempted to reduce all the varied phenomena of nature to the single principle of a force that always manifests itself in opposite directions. Accordingly, nature must no longer be divided up into separate groups of phenomena, with a special kind of force for each — mechanical, chemical, electrical, vital — but in all must be seen the same force in various forms, the same unity in duality.... In thus making the idea of force the supreme principle of nature Schelling has manifestly stripped that conception of its purely mechanical connotation, and thus it becomes practically identical with the idea of nature as an eternal process or manifestation of self-activity."[3] Schelling took the aesthetic view of nature according to which reality was regarded as a living whole, as the expression through-out of spirit, the highest reach of thought and final attitude of speculation. Froebel likewise employed aesthetic metaphor to explain the relation of the world to God. Thus, he said, "The relation of nature to God may be truly and clearly perceived and recognised by man in the study and elucidation of the innermost spiritual relation of a genuine human work of art to the artist."[4]

Hegel's Idealism

In Hegel the idealism of Kant found its consummation and completest expression. For Hegel there is only one form of existence, the spiritual, and it comprises the natural. The ultimate source of all being and of all knowing is Mind or the Absolute. In introducing the couplet "The real is the rational and the rational is real" Hegel referred to Plato. "The Absolute," he explained, "is Mind (Spirit) — this is the supreme definition of the Absolute. To find this definition and to grasp its meaning and burden is, we may say, the ultimate purpose of all education and all philosophy."[5]

Hegel's Influence on Froebel

The opening paragraph of Froebel's *The Education of Man* expresses in vague terminology the Hegelian standpoint, "The whole world, the All, the Universe — is a single great organism in which an eternal Uniformity manifests itself. This principle of uniformity expresses itself as much in external nature as in spirit. Life is the union of the spiritual with the material. Without mind or spirit matter is lifeless, it remains formless, it is mere chaos. Only through the entrance of the spiritual into the material does the cosmos originate. Spirit manifests itself in order. Every creature, every object is matter informed by spirit.... God is the presupposition, the condition of their existence. Without God they would not exist. God is the one ground of all things. God is the all-comprehending, the all-sustaining. God is the essential nature, the meaning of the world."[6]

Hegelian Dialectic in Froebel's Writings

A transition into its opposite is the result of extending a conception beyond its legitimate sphere. This 'law of opposites' Froebel fully exploited when he said, "Everything and every being comes to be known only as it is connected with the opposite of its kind, and its unity, its agreement with its opposite, is discovered."[7] Opposites have nevertheless significance only within a more inclusive unit. Froebel exemplified Hegelian dialectical movement in his various writings, the child is a child of nature, a human child and a child of God.[8] Morality mediates between religion and practical efficency.[9] The selection of objects constituting the second gift is determined by the same principle. "The sphere and the cube are pure opposites. They stand to each other in the relation of unity and plurality, but especially of movement and rest, of round and straight. The law of connection demands for these two objects of play a connecting one, which is the cylinder. It combines unity complete in itself in the round surface, and plurality in the two straight ones."[10]

Influence of Krause

Froebel was acquainted and maintained a correspondence with Kráuse. Krause's writings and his acquaintance with Froebel had an influence upon the latter. Krause's writings even lent expression to Froebel's views, in formulating which the latter experienced much difficulty. For Krause, everything exists in God. The world is not however, God Himself, but it is only in and through God. Reason and nature are the two highest hemispheres of the world as they exist in God, bright and powerful as God's actual image and likeness. The life of reason is not lawless caprice nor the life of nature is dead necessity. In both are recognised divine freedom and beauty. There is parallelism between the power and works of nature and reason. This parallelism is necessary and abiding, because both nature and reason exhibit the same essential being of the Deity. Man is the living unity of the two. He is the most glorious part of the harmony of reason and nature which is established by God.

According to Baroness von Marenhlz-Bulow, "The theory in which Froebel and Krause agreed especially, is the idea of the analogy existing between organic development in nature and organic development in the spiritual world, and according to which the historical development of mankind had proceeded, obeying the same laws as those of nature and its organisms. The same logic of the one all penetrating Divine reason rules in both, unconscious in the one (nature), conscious to itself in the other (mind). Therefore are the opposites ruling everywhere, not absolute, but relative, and always find connection or solution in the process of life."[11]

Development of the Individual

Froebel maintains that the mind unfolds from within according to a predetermined pattern. "All the child is ever to be and become, lies, however slightly indicated, in the child, and can be attained only through development from within outward."[12] The pattern followed is that known as preformation according to which the germ contains in miniature the fully developed plant or animal, point for point. Thus in the pedagogies of the Kindergarten Froebel says, "The tree germ bears within itself the nature of the whole tree; the development and formation of the whole future life of each being is contained in the beginning of its existence."[13] The development of the individual also parallels the course of development of the race. "In the development of the inner life of the individual man the history of the spiritual development of the race is repeated." It is also a continuous process. "It is highly important," Froebel affirms, "that man's development should proceed continuously from one point, and that this continuous progress be seen and ever guarded. Sharp limits and definite sub-divisions within the continuous series of the years of development, withdrawing from attention the permanent continuity, the living connection, the inner living essence, are therefore highly pernicious, and even destructive in their influence."[14]

Aim of Education

The aim of education, according to Froebel, consists solely in so treating man as to awaken in him his spiritual nature. "Surely the nature of man is in itself good."[15] This derived from Rousseau's view of the innate goodness of the child. Its corollary for the early stages of development was negative education. If man's inner and divine nature is not marred by untoward external influences, the ideal of education would be passive and non-interfering. "Indeed, in its very essence, education should have these characteristics; for the undisturbed operation of the Divine Unity is necessarily good — cannot be otherwise than good."[16]

However, this ideal condition of affairs is seldom obtained. Froebel admits, "Nature rarely shows us that unmarred original state, especially in man; but it is for this reason only the more necessary to assume its existence in every human being until the opposite has been clearly shown; otherwise that unmarred original state where it might exist contrary to our expectation, might be easily impaired."[17] When it is clearly established that the original nature of the individual has been marred, then Froebel does not hesitate to prescribe categorical principles.

Like Kant's categorical imperative Froebel asserts, "In its inner essence the living thought, the eternal spiritual ideal, ought to be and is categorical and mandatory in its manifestations.... The ideal becomes mandatory only where it supposes that the person addressed enters into the reason of the requirement with serene, childlike faith, or with clear, manly insight. It is true, in word or example, the ideal is mandatory in all these cases, but always only with reference to the spirit and inner life, never with reference to outer form."[18]

Meaning of Freedom

As for Hegel freedom is the truth of necessity; so for Froebel "In good education, in genuine instruction, in true training, necessity should call forth freedom; law, self-determination; external compulsion, inner free-will; external hate, inner love. Where hatred brings forth hatred; law, dishonesty and crime; compulsion, slavery; necessity, servitude; where oppression destroys and debases; where severity and harshness give rise to stubbornness and deceit — all education is abortive. In order to avoid the latter and to secure the former, all prescription should be adapted to the pupil's nature and needs, and secure his cooperation. This is the case when all education in instruction and training, in spite of its necessarily categorical character, bears in all details and ramifications the irresistible impress that the one who makes the demand is himself strictly unavoidedly subject to an eternally ruling law, to an unavoidable eternal necessity, and that, therefore, all despotism is banished."

Stages of Development

The stages recognised by Froebel, namely, infancy, childhood, youth, corresponded to Rousseau's divisions in *The Emile.* For Rousseau the activity characteristic of infancy is habit; for Froebel it is sensory development. Froebel's account of sensory development is highly artificial, the result of an attempt to impose on it the dialectical form. Childhood, the second stage, is distinguished from infancy by the appearance of language; it is then the child begins to represent the internal outwardly. Actual education now begins, attention and watchful care, being less directed to the body than to the mind. Speech training should now begin. Each object should be given its appropriate name, and each word should be uttered clearly and distinctly. On pedagogical grounds Froebel supports Pestalozzi, maintaining that to the child names are still one with the thing, and that name creates the thing for the child. In *The Pedagogies of the Kindergarten* he maintains that the name defines the object by connecting it with something familiar.

Planning of Education

It is in treating of childhood in *The Education of Man* that Froebel formulates his plea for the significance of play in education. Play is the characteristic activity of childhood. "It is," says Froebel, "the highest phase of child development... of human development at this period; for it is self-active representation of the inner — from inner necessity and impulse. Play is the purest, most spiritual activity of man at this stage, and, at the same time, typical of human life as a whole — of the inner hidden natural life in man and all things. It gives, therefore, joy, freedom, contentment, inner and outer rest, peace with the world. It holds the source of all that is good."[19]

Guidance in Play

To have educative value, the play of the child must not be a purposeless activity. His play impulses must be directed and controlled by the use of definite material necessitating an orderly sequence in the feelings engendered and in the activities exercised. "Without rational, conscious guidance," Froebel said, "childish activity degenerates into aimless play instead of preparing for those tasks of life for which it is destined.... In the Kindergarten the children are guided to bring out their plays in such a manner as really to reach the aim desired by nature, that is, to serve for their development.... Human education needs a guide which I think I have found in a general law of development that rules both in nature and in the intellectual world. Without law-abiding guidance there is no free development."[20]

Law of Opposites

At the transition from childhood to boyhood, Froebel proposes an inversion. "Whereas the period of childhood is characterised as predominantly that of life for the sake of living, for making the internal external, the period of boyhood is predominantly the period of learning, for making the external internal."[21] Here we have an illustration of Froebel's law of opposites. Education is not to be endowment determined. It is to be environmentally determined. It is to be curriculum-centred. Actually it is both endowment and environmentally determined from the outset. In *The Pedagogies of the Kindergarten* Froebel virtually admits this through his recognition of a third or synthesising stage. "Another fundamental idea is that all knowledge and comprehension of life are connected with making the internal external, the external internal, and with perceiving the harmony and accord of both."[22]

Work in Boyhood

While play is the characteristic activity of childhood, work is that of boyhood. Interest in the process gives place to interest in the product. In the words of Froebel, "What formerly the child did for the sake of the activity, the boy now does for the sake of the result or product of his activity."[23] "If activity brought joy to the child, work now gives delight to the boy."[24] For while during the previous period of childhood the aim of play consisted simply in activity as such, the aim lies now in a definite, conscious purpose. This contrast is forced and invalid; work is regarded as directed and purposive, whereas, in disregard of Froebel's previous statements to play, play is now simply an 'activity as such.' The more extended range of the pupil's environment has provided him with new patterns of activity in the shape of vocational occupations to be imitated. For the boy these are another form on play, not work in the sense of his parent's work. The pupil's activities at the boyhood are neighbourhood occupations. His development is determined, by the widening range of environment rather than by a sudden transition from inner experience to outer. For Froebel there is a unity transcending the opposition between play and work, for both he regards as means to the individual's self-realisation. "Man works," he affirms, "only that his spiritual divine essence may assume outward form, and that he may be enabled to recognise his own spiritual, divine nature and the innermost being of God."[25]

Project Activities

The activities in which the boy engages have all the characteristics of projects — practical problems involving cooperative effort and affording intellectual and moral training. "If in his former activity (in childhood) he emulated phases of domestic life, in his present activity (in boyhood) he shares the work of the house — lifting, pulling, carrying, digging, splitting."[26] According to Schlipp, Froebel, particularly in his *Education of Man*, has given the world no mean anticipation of Dewey's own school.[27]

Instruction

The other main feature of boyhood education is instruction. It serves to mark the transition from making the internal external to making the external internal. "Instruction is conducted not so much in accordance with the nature of man as in accordance with the fixed, definite, clear laws in the nature of things, and more particularly the laws to which man and things are equally subject. It is conducted in accordance with fixed and definite conditio lying outside the human being."[28]

School Curriculum

In describing his pupil's life and education from the development standpoint Froebel proposes various educational occupations and expounds his attitude to these. The subjects are not to be regarded as ends in themselves; they are merely instrumental to the full realisation of the pupil's personality. Through it he comes to himself. "Every child, boy and youth, whatever his condition or position in life, should devote daily at least one or two hours to some serious activity in the production of some definite external piece of work.... Children — mankind, indeed — are at present too much and too variously concerned with aimless and purposeless pursuits, and too little with work. Children and parents consider the activity of actual work so much to their disadvantage, and so unimportant for their future conditions of life, that educational institutions should make it one of their most constant endeavours to dispel this delusion. The domestic and scholastic education of our time leads children to indolence and laziness; a vast amount of human power thereby remains undeveloped and is lost."[29]

Other Subjects

Froebel also recommends the introduction of such subjects as drawing, nature study and school gardening. He insists on an all-round development of the aim of education. As the main divisions of an educational curriculum he enumerates : (i) religion and religious instruction, (ii) natural science and mathematics, (iii) language and (iv) art and objects of art. Human education requires the knowledge and appreciation of religion, nature and language with reference to the aim of instruction in art, for Froebel states, "Its intention will not be to make each pupil an artist in some one or all of the arts, but to secure to each human being full and all-sided development."[30]

The Kindergarten

Froebel devoted the later part of his life to founding the Kindergarten on which his fame mainly rests. The name 'Kindergarten' came to Froebel one spring day in 1840 as with some friends he was proceeding from Keilhau to Bankendrug when from a hill he saw the valley of the Rinne, a tributary of the Saale, stretching out before him like a great garden and exclaimed, "I have found it. Kindergarten shall the name be." It was not till 1843 that the institution of the Kindergarten was founded, though date usually given is 1840.

Froebel considered "childhood as the most important stage of the total development of man and humanity."[31] In his *Reminiscences* he gives his reason then, "The earliest age is the most important one for education, because the beginning decides the manner of progress and the end. If national order is to be recognised in later years as a benefit, childhood must first be accustomed to law and order, and therein find means of freedom."[32] For this stage of childhood, Froebel elaborated his gifts, the first being the ball, the second the sphere, the cube and the cylinder.

Gifts and Occupations

In his gifts Froebel personifies playthings and assumes that children will be able to appreciate the symbolism involved. He also believes that the quasi-philosophic conceptions which underline the games will impress themselves on the child's mind and determine his attitude to life. He was so obsessed with his philosophical formulae that his psychological insight could not save him from such absurdities as assuming that the child when dealing with the second gift, that is, during the second half of the first year of his life, has some dim perception of the nature and destiny of man. In his account of the same play, he affirms man himself "in play, even as a child, by play should perceive within and without how from unity proceed manifoldness, plurality, and totality, and how plurality and manifoldness finally are found again in and resolve themselves into unity and should find this out in life."[33] In reviewing the first plays he observes, "In and by means of the ball (as an object resting in itself, easily movable, especially elastic, bright, and warm) the child perceives his life, his power, his activity, and that of his senses, at the first stage of his consciousness, in their unity, and thus exercises them.... The ball is therefore to the child a representative or a means of perception of a single effect caused by a single power. The sphere is to the child the representative of every isolated simple unity; the child gets a hint in the sphere of the manifoldness as still abiding in unity. The cube is to the child the representative of each continually developing manifold body. The child has an intimation in it of the unity which lies at the foundation of all manifoldness and from which the latter proceeds. In sphere and cube, considered in comparison with each other, is presented an outward view of the child, the resemblance between opposites which is so important for his whole future life, and which he perceives everywhere around himself, and multifariously within himself."[34]

By his methodological arrangement of the gifts and occupations Froebel founded a new type of educational institution. Although his system too readily lent itself to formalism by later generations of teachers who had not the spirit of the master, it ameliorated the lot of countless children. His theory is also open to criticism. In the ground of its excessive symbolism, to conclude with Dewey "Froebel's recognition of significance of the native capacities of children, his loving attention to them, and his influence in inducing others to study them, represents perhaps the most effective single force in modern educational theory in effecting widespread acknowledgement of the idea of growth."[35]

REFRENCES

1. *Autobiography of Freidrich Froebel*, p. 107.
2. *Ibid.*
3. J. Watson, *Schelling's Transcendental Idealism* (Chicago : S.C. Griggs & Co.), pp. 95-96.
4. Froebel, *The Education of Man*, p. 153.
5. W. Wallace, *Hegel's Philosophy of Mind* (Oxford University Press, 1894), p. 7.
6. F. Froebel, *The Education of Man*, translated by W.N. Hailman (New York : D. Appleton & Co., 1990).
7. *Ibid.*, p. 42.
8. *The Pedagogies of the Kindergarten*, translated by Josephine Jarvis (London : Edward Arnold & Co., 1900), p. 11.
9. *The Education of Man*, ch. I.
10. *Education by Development*, the second part of *The* Pedagogies *of the Kindergarten* translated by Josephine Jarvis (New York : D. Appleton & Co., 1905), p. 204.
11. *Reminiscences*, p. 248.
12. *The Education of Man*, p. 68.
13. *Op. cit.*, pp. 5-6.
14. *The Education of Man*, p. 27.
15. *Ibid.*, p. 120.
16. *Ibid.*, pp. 7-8.
17. *Ibid.*, p. 9.
18. *Ibid.*, p. 13.
19. *Ibid.*, p. 55.
20. *Reminiscences*, pp. 67-68.
21. *Ibid.*, p. 94.
22. *Op. cit.*, p. 174.

23. *Ibid.*, p. 99.
24. *Ibid.*, p. 102.
25. *Ibid.*, p. 112.
26. *Ibid.*, pp. 101, 106, 113.
27. *The Philosophy of John Dewey* (Evanston : Northwestern University Press, 1939), p. 453.
28. Froebel, *The Education of Man*, pp. 94-95.
29. *Ibid.*, pp. 34-35.
30. *Ibid.*, p. 228.
31. *The Pedagogies of the Kindergarten*, p. 95.
32. *Reminiscences*, p. 143.
33. *The Pedagogies of the Kindergarten*, p. 98.
34. *Ibid.*, p. 105.
35. Dewey, *Democracy and Education*, pp. 67-68.

7

J.F. HERBART
(1776-1841)

Psychological Approach

According to Herbart, "Pedagogy as a science is based on practical philosophy and on psychology. The former points out the aim of culture, the latter the way, the means and the obstacles."[1] In *Observations of a Pedagogical Essay* Herbart further explains, "I have for twenty years employed metaphysics, mathematics, and side by side with them self-observation, experience and experiments, merely to find the foundations of true psychological insight. And the motive for these not entirely effortless investigations has been, and is, in the main my conviction that a large part of the enormous gaps in our pedagogical knowledge results from lack of psychology."[2]

Negative or Critical Psychology

Herbart disposed of both mental faculties and formal training. His uncompromising polemic against innate faculties, activities and predispositions is the most striking negative feature of his psychology. "The soul," says Herbart, "has no innate tendencies nor faculties." Again, "It is an error, indeed, to look upon the human soul as an aggregate of all sorts of faculties. The faculties are, indeed, nothing real, but merely logical designations for the preliminary classification of psychical phenomena."[3]

Training of the Faculties

In his *Brief Encyclopaedia of Practical Philosophy* Herbart remarks, "Those, however, who have no proper psychological insight seldom grasp anything about the rules of education. They cling to the old idea that there are certain powers or faculties in the soul which have to be exercised, and it does not matter what they are exercised on. The exercises might well belong to the same category as gymnastic exercises, because men have only one kind of muscle, and by gymnastics the muscles of the body become strong and pliable. In actual fact every apperceptive system comprises elements of imagination, memory and reason, though naturally not all in equal proportions. In one and the same person there can quite easily be, and usually there is, an apperceptive system composed predominantly of intellectual elements, while another is rich in imagination, while in a third memory plays the greatest part. Intense feeling may colour one apperceptive system, whereas apathy characterises another. What educators call formal training is accordingly a complete chimera, since it presupposes the exercise of powers existing only in the imagination of those who hold such views on psychology." According to the assumption, mental powers cannot work in isolation.

Unity of Mental Life

Herbart has been credited by Merz of preserving the unity of mental life for the psychologists who have been influenced by him. "Thus, it is a characteristic of all psycho-physical writers who have come under the influence of Herbart, that however much they may be occupied with detailed description of physiological processes, with the analysis of sensations, or the direction of the data of experience, they never lost night of the underlying mental unity which is the central phenomenon of psychology and of psycho-physics, just as it must be the central problem of biology to arrive at some definition of life.... It seems to me that, in Germany at least, it is through Herbart, more than through any other thinker, that we have been preserved from a threatening disintegration of psychological research."[4]

Nature of Soul

The simple nature of the soul, according to Herbart, is totally unknown. It is as little an object of speculative as of empirical psychology. In so far as the soul is endowed with the power of presentation, it may be regarded as mind. In Herbart's psychological investigation the abstract metaphysical unity of the soul becomes transformed into a concrete unity pervading and connecting the manifold variety of individual experience. That passions or feelings arise from ideas. Satisfaction or uneasiness is associated with thought. Feelings are but passing modifications of the existing presentations. "Feelings and desires are conditions, and for the most part changeable conditions of presentation."

In the mental life when a presentation meets with a presentation opposed to it, an unpleasant feeling results. But pleasure results if its realisation is facilitated.

Intellectualism

The intellectualism of Herbart's psychology is intensified by his use of the term 'Empfindungen' to signify both sensation and feeling. In the *Introduction to the Allegemeine Padagogik* he says that out of thoughts arise feelings (Empfindungen), and, from those principles and mode of action. According to Herbart, the circle of thought is no mere intellectual structure. It is interwoven throughout with feelings and volitional impulses. The task of educative instruction is to anchor this circle of thought.

Dependence of Emotion on Ideals

Herbart's view of the dependence of emotion on ideas has important educational consequences. There can be no education of the feelings *per se*. Herbart was not content to rely on the emotionalism of Rousseau or the sentimentalism of Pestalozzi for moral training. He demanded a surer foundation. He found it in 'the circle of thought.' He said, "The disposition of the heart has its source in the mind."

The Herbartian system of ideas for "presentations must be regarded as forces whose effectiveness depends upon their strength, their oppositions and their combinations, all of which are different in degree." Herbart's doctrine of psychical mechanism has become the common possession of scientific psychologists. He diverted attention from mental contents to mental activities or forces, to the interaction among presentations. Instead of viewing the mental life as a succession of states of consciousness or as a stream of consciousness he conceived it as a mental system.

Role of Subjective Factors

Herbart's main contribution to psychology is the emphasis he lays on the part subjective factors play in the mental process. Thus to account for perception we have to assume reinstated or revived experiences constituting the precept. In perception this coalescing is known as assimilation or compilation.

Apperception

Apperception is an analogous process on a higher level. It is the interpretation of a precept by a system of ideas. In the words of Herbart, "Apperception or assimilation takes place through the reproduction of previously acquired presentations and their union with the new element". It implies the dependence of the new on the old, of the interpretation of the new by the old, it is not confined to sense-perception but embraces 'inner perception' as well. Once presentation-mass may exert a determining influence on another. Thus what we notice depends not so much on the strength of the external stimulus or on the susceptibility of the subject as on the context, the mental system dominant at the time. This accounts for the fact that different people or the same person at different times have dirrerent perceptions under the same external conditions. As Herbart remarks, "Even in the same surroundings every man has own world." Thus apperception emphasises the significant part that old knowledge plays in the acquisition of the new knowledge which should always be a development of previous knowledge.

Aim of Education

Although psychology provides the means, philosophy dictates the end of education. While Herbart confesses that education has no time to take holiday till philosophical questions are once for all cleared up,[5] he admits, "To teach completely how life is determined by its two rulers, Speculation and Taste, we must seek for a system of philosophy, the keystone of instruction"[6] and he also claims that the true perception of education is philosophy.[7]

In the opening sentences of *Dissertation on the Aesthetic Description of the World as the main function of Education* Herbart affirms, "The one and the whole work of education may be summed up in the concept — morality." But he goes on to explain, "I therefore, believe that the mode of consideration which places morality at the head is the most important, but not the only and comprehensive standpoint of education."[8] He regards an aesthetic interpretation of the world as the ideal of education.[9]

Exaltation of Personality

Neither ethics nor aesthetics, can, however, determine fully the end of education. Education must include the ideals of truth and righteousness as well as of goodness and beauty. Intellectual inquiry and religious reverence are as natural to man and as necessary to him for the full realisation of his personality as are ethical and aesthetic enjoyment. The aim of education as of life itself cannot be formulated in any more succinct phrase tham of Eucken, namely to exalt personality. According to Herbart, we need not go beyond experience to see that there is a great diversity in intellectual talents. The educability of the child is limited by his individuality. In the *Minor Pedagogical Works*, he says that it is a chief requisite of a good pedagogical plan that it be flexible enough to fit the various capacities.[10]

Herbart, however, seeks to avoid that individuality should develop into eccentricity. Where this occurs, a state of society results in which each brags of his own individuality, and no one understands his fellows.[11] Hence Herbart does not make the development of individuality the aim of education. Individuality is one of the data of education, not the end. It has to be fashioned into personality. This is achieved through the development of a variety of interests and their integration.

The Aspects of Human Activity

Human activity, for Herbart, has two main aspects; many-sided interest and moral character. Many-sided interest is further qualified by 'evenly balanced.' This is equivalent to the popular statement — the harmonious expansion of all the powers of the individual. Many-sidedness is opposed not only to one-sidedness but also the discursiveness. It must be distinguished from its exaggeration — dabbling in many things.

Two Aspects of Interest

Interest has two aspects — a subjective or psychological and an objective. The objective aspect comprises the various activities in which the individual participates or the different aspects of the environment to which he reacts. It consists of two main divisions : (i) knowledge and (ii) sympathy, although Herbart explains that the environment of objects for knowledge embraces nature and humanity and that only certain expressions of humanity belong to what he terms sympathy.

Divisions of Knowledge

Herbart divides knowledge into (1) actual phenomena, (2) scientific laws and (3) aesthetic relations (or the empirical, the speculative and the aesthetic), representing different attitudes to our natural environment or different aspects of experience. He divides sympathy into (1) human, (2) social and (3) religious, representing different attitudes in social intercourse or different aspects of our spiritual environment. These constitute the six facets of a many-sided interest. When properly exploited they provided a liberal training or an all-round education.

The Sources of Presentation

Presentation masses emanate from two main sources — experience and social intercourse. Through experience we acquire knowledge, and through intercourse we develop sympathy. While we cannot dispense with experience and intercourse, they must be supplemented by instruction, for, as Herbart claims, experience seems to expect that instruction will follow how to analyse the material which she has amassed and to collect and arrange her scattered and formless fragments. To sum up, "Interest arises from interesting objects and occupations. Many-sided interest originates in the wealth of these. To create and develop this interest is the task of instruction which carries on and completes the preparation begun by intercourse and experience."[12] Instruction alone, adds Herbart, can lay claim to cultivate a well-balanced, all embracing many-sidedness.[13] It is for this reason that Herbart keeps reiterating that he has no conception of education without instruction; conversely, he does not acknowledge any instruction which does not educate.[14]

Value of Instruction

Herbart says, "The chief means of positive education lies in instruction taken in its widest sense."[15] Not all instruction is, however, educative. The types of instruction which are not educative are those which afford only temporary pleasure or light entertainment, and such studies as remain isolated do not lead to continued effort.

Two Forms of Instruction

Instruction may take two main forms — synthetic and analytic. The child's experience may be augmented. This is narrative instruction. It has but one law — to describe in such a way that the pupil believes he sees what is described.[16] Or the teacher may avail himself of the pupil's experience eliciting the facts which he requires for his exposition. These facts require to be organised according to the purpose the teacher has in view. Both these forms of exposition — narrative and educative — are classed by Herbart as synthetic. The pupil's experience may not only be inadequate, it may even be erroneous. In this case the teacher must dissect it to utilise the elements in a new systematic whole. This Herbart terms analytic instruction. He adds, "The pupil ought properly to provide the materials for analytic instruction, especially in later years."[17] The various forms of presentation or exposition are not mutually exclusive, but may be combined in the same lesson as occasion requires. In his *Science of Education* Herbart illustrates how the analytic and synthetic types of instruction may by employed in the respective fields of interests — empirical, scientific, aesthetic, human, social and religious.[18] But his treatment is too general to provide a curriculum which must arrange the opportunities provided in accordance with the needs of the pupils and the individual powers of the teacher. Earlier, Herbart had suggested the principle of recapitulation as a guide to the organisation of teaching material. This doctrine plays a prominent part in Herbartian literature. He said, "If pupils would continue the work of their forefathers they must have travelled the same way; above all, they must have learned to recognise these forefathers as their own from their early years."[19]

Doctrine of Interest

The interests which constitute the main divisions of education are interests of one person. Herbart warns us, "Do not forget interest among interesting things."[20] It is with the doctrine of interest in this sense, that Herbart's name has come to be associated in Britain and in America.

According to Herbart, "The word interest stands in general for that kind of mental activity which it is the business of instruction to create. Mere information does not suffice, for this we think of as a supply or store of facts which a person might possess or lack, and still remain the same being. But he who lays hold of his information and reaches out more, takes an interest in it."

Interest is thus a concomitant of mental activity. "Interest," he says, "means self-activity. But not all self-activity, only the right degree of the right kind, is desirable, else lively children might very well be left to themselves. There would be no need of educating or controlling them. It is the purpose of instruction to give the right direction to their thoughts and impulses, to incline these towards the morally good and true. Interest is opposed to indifference. It displays a preference over mere perception for certain objects by arousing in the mind analogous presentations and involuntarily suppressing others. It differs from certain other mental processes by depending on its object and referring to the present."[21]

It should not be confused with amusement. "The teacher," says Herbart, "should not be misled into turning instruction into play, nor designedly into work; he sees before him a serious business and tries to forward it with gentle but steady hand."[22] That which is too simple must be avoided. "Instruction must be comprehensible and yet difficult rather than easy, otherwise it causes ennui."[23]

Interest depends partly on native capacity which the school cannot create; but it depends also on the subject-matter of instruction, and also on its arrangement. We must know both what to teach and how to teach it.

When presentations arise spontaneously in the pupil's mind, the pupils are said to be attentive and the instruction has an interest for them. When attention has to be enforced, it is doubtful whether an interest in the subject can ever be evoked. As Herbart explains, "Presentations that must by effort be raised into consciousness because they do not rise spontaneously, may become spontaneous by gradual strengthening. But this development we cannot count on unless instruction, advancing step by step, bring it about."

Knowledge is likewise likely to be inanimate if it remains detached or dissociated from a general system of ideas. Herbart warns us, "If the facts of knowledge are allowed to fall asunder... instruction endangers the whole of education."

Concentration and Co-ordination

No matter what subject matter is selected or what method of exposition is adopted, the same sequence must be followed in instruction if interest is to ensure. Herbart insisted that teaching procedure should be adapted to the stages discernible in the development of knowledge. He first distinguished two phases — an intensive and an extensive : *Vertiefung* — absorption in or concentration on a subject and *Besinnung* — co-ordination and systematisation, of the results of *Vertiefung*.[24] In one of his

Aphorisms, Herbart explains that *Vertiefung* or concentration occurs when a thought to dominate the mind that it suppresses the ordinary contents of consciousness, and *Besinnung* — coordination when these ordinary contents re-establish themselves; coordination is essential not only to collect and combine the defects of concentration but also to prevent a lop-sided development.[25]

As these two concepts are too general for practical purposes Herbart finds it necessary to subdivide concentration into clearness and association, and coordination into system and method. Clearness, association system and method thus become Herbart's formal steps in teaching.[26]

"In order always to maintain the mind's coherence," Herbart argues, "instruction must follow the rule of giving equal weight in every smallest possible group of its objects to concentration and reflection; that is to say, it must care equally and in regular succession for clearness of every particular, for association of the manifold, for coherent ordering of what is associated, and for a certain practice in progression through this order. Upon this depends the distinctness which must rule in all that is taught."[27]

Under clearness Herbart includes the analysis and synthesis of the given. Through association the new knowledge presented to the pupil is connected with the old. It implies the apperceptive process. It is analogous to the preparation stage of the Herbartian five formal steps. Its purpose is to secure a proper orientation of the subject to be taught. "For Association," Herbart tells us, "the best mode of procedure is informal conversation, because it gives the pupil an opportunity to test and to change the accidental union of his thoughts, to multiply the links of connection, and to assimilate, after his own fashion, what he has learned. It enables him, besides, to do at least a part of all this in any way that happens to be the easiest and most convenient. Association prepares the way for system, which is the perfect order of a copious coordination." "By exhibiting and emphasising the leading principles," Herbart adds, "system impresses upon the minds of pupils the value of organised knowledge." In the generally accepted Herbartian tradition, system is termed generalisation. A system is not to be merely learned, it is to be used, applied and often needs to be supplemented by additions inserted at appropriate places. This application Herbart terms method.

Herbart's formal steps apply to method-wholes, instructional units or centres of interest, not to individual lessons. They are stages in the exposition of a topic which has a unity and completeness in itself. It was the mechanical application of the formal steps in each and every lesson that brought the Herbartian method into discredit.

Interest and Desire

In introducing the concept of many-sidedness of interest, Herbart believed that one aspect of human activity was being neglected, namely, action and what immediately impels thereto — desire.[28] The two spheres of human activity are accordingly interest and desire, knowing and willing. They are nevertheless not unconnected, being linked through instruction.

Circle of Thought

Just as instruction creates a many-sided interest, so it has also the task of developing 'the circle of thought'. The section dealing with the influence of the circle of thought on character is the central point of the Science of Education.[29] It is the vantage point from which the whole should be viewed.

According to Herbart, the chief seat of the cultivation of character lies in the circle of thought and that in it lies the main part of education.[30]

Character tainting is unable to accomplish its work unless in conjunction with instruction. It will be seen when the task of setting forth the whole of virtue is renewed in its completeness that the main things are accomplished by instruction. In the *Introduction to the Science of Education*, Herbart affirms, "Those only wield the full power of education who know how to cultivate in the youthful soul a large circle of thought closely connected in all its parts, possessing the power of overcoming that which is unfavourable in the environment, and of dissolving and absorbing into itself all that is favourable."[31] In his reply to Jackmann's review Herbart repeats, "Instruction will above all form the circle of thought and education the character. The latter is nothing without the former — herein is contained the whole sum of my pedagogy." In his *Brief Encyclopaedia* Herbart takes credit for introducing the term 'an educative instruction'. The principle of the determination of the inner aspect of character by means of instruction is Herbart's chief contribution to educational thought. "Moral education," he sums up, "is not separable from education as a whole."[32]

Value of Will

While instruction is thus the central theme of Herbart's doctrine he never allows us to forget that man's worth does not lie in his knowing but in his willing. He is however, against all constraint upon moral will. "It may be doubted," he explains, "whether the treatment of discipline in the sense of constraint belongs to pedagogy or should not more appropriately be appended to those parts of practical philosophy which treat of government in general."[33] Moral improvement is not brought about by that constraint of government. Education can only begin after control has done its work. Later on Herbart nevertheless concedes that control may have both an indirect and a direct bearing on character; it partly helps to make that instruction possible which will influence the subsequent formation of character, and it serves to create through action or inaction a beginning of character.[34]

Control or Constraint

Control or constraint need not be repressive. Herbart reviews the various means of keeping order — supervision, the threat of punishment and compulsion. He concludes, "When the environment is so arranged that childish activity can of itself find the road to the useful and expend itself thereon, then control is most successful."[35]

Control or constraint is a necessary evil, doubtless better than anarchy, but its defect is that it weakens while education seeks to strengthen. It is negative and inhibitive, whereas education should be positive and purposive. Herbart's distinction between good behaviour secured by administrative regulations and gentlemanly conduct exercised by voluntary self-restraint has much significance in education.

Stages in Character Training

Corresponding to the four formal steps in intellectual instructions are the four stages in character training; these are *Merken* (to imprint), *Erwarten* (to anticipate), *Forden* (to desire), *Handeln* (to act). Although Herbart affirms that character is the embodiment of the will, he does not include the will as a separate function among the subjective aspects of character training. The will, for him, is not something apart from desire; 'action generates the will out of desire.'[36] The teacher's task is to assist the pupil to acquire the right desire, for when opportunity presents itself and the pupil realises that he can attain his end, action follows, "will is desire combined with the consciousness of the attainment of what is desired."[37]

To conclude with Robert R. Rusk, "Educators previous to the time of Herbart had made the training of character the end of education while others had recognised the importance of instruction, but it was left to Herbart to connect instruction with character training through interest and to prove techniques based on psychological considerations for the attainment of both. He made the proper selection of the content of instruction and the right method of presenting the selected content, moral duties incumbent on the teacher, and contributing to the achievement of the aim which he set up for himself."[38]

REFRENCES

1. J.F. Herbart, *Outlines of Educational Doctrine* (New York : The Macmillan Co., 1901).
2. Herbart, *ABC of Sense Perception and Minor Pedagogical Works*, p. 72.
3. *Ibid.*
4. J.T. Merz, *A History of European Thought in the Nineteenth Century*, Vol. II, pp. 496-500 (Edinburgh : W. Blackwood & Sons, 1896-1914).

5. *The Science of Education*, p. 108.
6. *Ibid.*, p. 195.
7. *Minor Pedagogical Works*, p. 151.
8. *The Science of Education*, p. 108.
9. *Minor Pedagogical Works*, p. 16.
10. *Op. cit.*, p. 181.
11. *The Science of Education*, p. 142.
12. *Ibid.*, p. 120.
13. *Ibid.*
14. *Ibid.*
15. *Aphorismen*, XXI.
16. *The Science of Education*, p. 155.
17. *Ibid.*, p. 187.
18. *The Science of Education*, pp. 170-86.
19. *Ibid.*, p. 165.
20. *Ibid.*, p.132.
21. *The Science of Education*, pp. 126-29.
22. *Ibid.*, p. 192.
23. *Ibid.*, p. 238.
24. *The Science of Education*, pp. 123-28.
25. *Aphorismen*, I
26. *The Science of Education*, p. 126.
27. *Ibid.*, pp. 144-45.
28. *Ibid.*, p. 129.
29. *Ibid.*, pp. 209-10.
30. *Ibid.*, pp. 214-220.
31. *Ibid.*, p.92.
32. *Ibid.*, p. 94.
33. *Ibid.*
34. *Ibid.*, p. 99.
35. *Ibid.*, p. 101.
36. *Ibid.*, p. 212.
37. *Ibid.*
38. Robert R. Rusk, *The Doctrines of The Great Educators* (London MacMillan, 1954), p. 237.

8

BERTRAND RUSSELL

(1872-1970)

Bertrand Russell was born in Trellock, Wales on May 18, 1872. His parents died when he was only three years of age. His grandparents brought him up. After attaining proficiency in German and French through a private tutor in home, in 1890, he took admission in Trinity College, Cambridge. Because of his interest in Philosophy he got first division with distinction. In 1894, he joined French Embassy in England and in 1895 he was appointed as a Fellow of Trinity College in recognition of his valuable contributions. He had special interest in Mathematics also. He was very much interested in the work of Italian mathematician Peano, and after studying his work, he published *Principles of Mathematics* in 1903. In 1910, he was appointed a Professor in Trinity College.

In the First World War, he took part in 'No Conscription Fellowship'. As a result he was fined one hundred pounds and his personal library was confiscated for non-payment of fine. He had also to leave his post as a Professor consequent to this punishment. On account of his outstanding abilities he was offered teaching work in Harvard. But the British Government denied him passport for going to Harvard.

In recognition of his rare excellence in intellectual pursuits he was awarded Nobel Prize for literature in 1950. On February 2, 1970, the intellectual world lost one of its most distinguished members when Russell died peacefully in his ninety-eighth year.

Bertrand Russell was a versatile and enchanting writer. His range was virtually encyclopaedic and he wrote on topics ranging from abstruse mathematical philosophy, popular science, logical studies, history of philosophy and socio-ethical and educational topics. His style was very simple and lucid. He enlightened lay persons about extremely complex topics by his thorough grasp of the subject-matter and gift of simple expression.

PHILOSOPHICAL APPROACH

The philosophy of Russell is based upon logic. Russell was never dogmatic. He was open to vary his opinions on ethical, epistemological and social philosophy in the light of growing knowledge. Therefore, his philosophical ideology does not fit into any traditional philosophical categories like idealism or realism. He christens his philosophy "logical positivism." He believes that a strict logical analysis is the appropriate approach to delve into Reality. His philosophy is a mix of mathematics and metaphysics and his social thinking is reformist. He makes a forceful plea for the removal of social constraints in order to promote creative thinking. He has devoted all his energies to the welfare of mankind. He considers social harmony and international peace as *sine qua non* of all human progress. He is opposed to each and every form of warfare. He vehemently believes that war can, under no circumstances, be justified. He helped organise world scientific community to raise a powerful voice against nuclear weaponry.

AIM OF EDUCATION

It is not an easy task to determine what is the true purpose of education. While some educational philosophers lay stress upon 'humbleness of mind,' others emphasize 'magnanimous man.' Some other philosophers variously emphasize character formation, learning, developing courage or moral rectitude and compassion. The *weltanschauung* or world-view of philosophers determines differences in their outlook on education. According to Russell, the aim of education is twofold — the development of noble individual and a society making the growth of nobility of man possible. However, it is problematic what may be considered good social organization and whom we should regard a good man.

According to Russell, the modern democratic societies can grow only if these are based upon the rock-like foundation of science. In the absence of scientific temper social values would stultify and become unprogressive. Therefore, Russell rejected the orthodoxy in education.

In the opinion of Bertrand Russell it must be granted that the intelligentsia of China was lazy and dedicated to leisurely pursuits whereas the Japanese intelligentsia was prone to dogmatism which is undesirable as this leads to upheaval in society.

Similarly the Jesuits also removed the child from the central position in education. The education under Jesuit dispensation aimed to make individuals subordinate to the interests of Catholic Church. But this attitude is unacceptable to modern man.

The system of education prevalent in England was a gift of the philosophy of Dr. Arnold. This education is aimed at the exclusive betterment of a particular class, namely, aristocracy. The values which protected the interests of privileged class were only promoted. Such an education did make young men hardy, efficient and healthy but they became slave of a particular set of beliefs. Consequently, the values of freedom of thought, power of imagination, compassion and tolerance were sacrificed as these militated against the interests of aristocracy. Firmness of intellectual prowess, toughness of character do not accord with humanism.

In the field of modern education, America occupies the top place. The American education is based upon fundamental principles and is also eminently practical. The physical and technological progress achieved in America makes it possible to make novel and innovative experiments. However, in America too much emphasis is laid upon nationalism and patriotism. While it is universally considered that to produce patriotic citizens is the valid aim of education, but, according to Russell, overemphasis on this ideal encourages bigotry and militates against world peace and harmony. Moreover, the best education is directed toward man and considers him as an end. The flowering of a child's talents and initiative must be the *summum bonum* of all education and any attempt to treat the child as a means to some external end, however glorious, must be decried.

If the welfare of child is the ultimate goal of all educational endeavour, then the teacher who is the pivot of education must love his pupils more than anything else. If the teacher considers his own ideals and patriotic feelings more vital than the child, he cannot help either to form the true character of his pupils or ignite their intelligence. And this type of affection can be present in the teacher if he regards the child as the supreme entity in the educational framework and does not allow it to become subservient to any other fact or value, however noble it may be in his estimation. A teacher should love children as much as if they were his own. However, this is not enough. He must be aware of what constitutes human excellence. He must be able to inculcate in children qualities that promote humanism and international harmony and discourage all those traits which are inimical to it. It is not possible to provide a uniform curriculum which will help growth of great intellectuals, scientists, artists and engineers but we should aim at the development of those traits which are essential to each of these categories of persons. Some qualities are such as must be universally present.

It is not easy to enumerate these common features. None the less we shall discuss below the four traits which Bertrand Russell considers to be essential in all civilised human beings. These are : (1) Vitality, (2) Courage, (3) Sensitiveness and (4) Intelligence.

1. Vitality. Vitality, vigour or keenness in life and spontaneous pleasure in simple and relative indifference to pain is optimally present in children. It is symptomatic of vigorous physical health and keen intelligence. It tapers off with age, but according to Russell, given the proper physical environment, social and intellectual milieu, it need not decline with growing age. It is not uncommon to find a number of vigorous and keenly intelligent old people. However, according to Russell, excessive materialism, acquisitive habits and wrong education sap this vitality. We must beware and ward off the malignant tendencies.

2. Courage. It is not easy to define courage; it is not possible to give a positive description of this quality. It can at best be defined negatively. In one word, courage is absence of fear. One can be unafraid only if he is utterly truthful and harbours no ill-will, envy or jealousy; to stand steadfast in the face of adversity and not to lose nerve and reason and become livid and timorous in the face of hazards like fire, storm, social violence and attack on one's person. Only those who lack fear can keep their cool and not become hysteric. Education should inculcate quality of fearlessness among children.

3. Sensitiveness. We naturally dislike blame and appreciate social approbation. A sensitive child is a sympathetic person who feels directly the pain or pleasure of others. As he feels offended by undue blame and enjoys appreciation and approval, he should avoid blaming others but extend hearty approval when they act well. To be sensitive is to be positively alive and to become indifferent is to invite ennui and listlessness. Thus, education must help children develop keen sensitivity.

4. Intelligence. The cultivation of intelligence is the norm of all systems of education. In spite of varying emphases and ideological differences, all educators are agreed upon the fact of developing child's intelligence. However, by intelligence we do not imply an acquisition of a body of knowledge or a storehouse of information lent an aptitude or keenness to learn. The education should enkindle curiosity in children and a desire to learn by self-exploration rather than stuffing the mind with chokeful of information. It is the curiosity which enables a child to grasp and assimilate knowledge, a mere collection of facts which are not systematised or made an active instrument of learning.

According to Russell, turning the inherent curiosity in desirable directions should be the aim of education. The curiosity can make knowledge wholesome and pleasant. The best technique of knowledge is to tap the curiosity in the child. The acquisition of knowledge presupposes certain conditions which are the habit of keen observation, patience, perseverance and an abiding faith in the possibility to know. These pristine qualities are self-generating and auto-propelled means of all useful and abstruse learning. These constitute the creative impulse, the fire within which set aflame and germinate all worthwhile knowing and discovery. Besides, an open-minded sensitive turn of mind is the jumping board of excellence in knowledge.

According to Bertrand Russell if the above-mentioned characteristics are realized through education, a peculiar sense of happiness and fulfilment dawns upon man. Bertrand Russell favours a holistic education satisfying the cognitive, affective and conative impulses of man.

GENERAL PRINCIPLES

According to Bertrand Russell first six years of a child are of critical importance. It is during this period that all the major traits which form the foundation of the character of the child are imprinted. For the formation of sound character, proper rearing and upkeep of the child are very essential.

According to Russell, after the age of six, the child should be exposed to exclusive intellectual training. To emphasize morality and idealism in education pre-eminently to the exclusion of rational and free thinking leads to a stagnant conformist personality and this is detrimental to excellence in thought and character. To make traditional morality a sacred cow, according to Bertrand Russell, stultifies the personality of children. All education imparted to children should have only twin ideals of satisfaction of the inherent curiosity and teaching the art of self-education and independent thinking. The teacher should only create an atmosphere which would stimuiate the child to think for himself and satisfy his curiosity by personal initiative and original technique; he should be made to desist from aping and gullible acceptance of what is told to him. It is quite possible that a child may not be satisfied by the routine curriculum in which case the teacher should suggest him ways and means which the child can try in his spare hours. Should a child try to know and try what is against received views and moral ideals of the society, the child should not be encouraged to adopt libertarian and non-conformist behaviour but at the same time his curiosity should not be nipped in bud by over sermonizing. Under no circumstances, the child should feel that he must fall in line with the views of elders to become acceptable to society. All those who have helped society to become more civilized and creative have thought ideas which were ahead of their times and unacceptable to their contemporary social and cultural institutions. For example, if a child should become interested in erotic literature and erotic audio-visual materials, a normal response is to punish him and make him realize his guilt and immorality. But, according to Bertrand Russell, such an approach would be counter-productive. The proper approach is to make, the child feel normal and given sex education in an objective manner so that the salacious matter no longer overwhelms him. If the child is enlightened about sexuality he would not be misled or become secretive in sexual matters. To overawe the child with moral horror of sex would not keep the child protected from exposure to sexual stimuli but would only create in him a feeling of guilt. This would in all probability make him a sadist or masochist. In the case of obsessive preoccupation with sex, the child needs to be treated psychologically and clinically. His sickness should be treated as we would treat cold or pneumonia. The proper development of intelligence requires, according to Russell, following qualities — (1) Curiosity, (2) Open-mindedness, (3) Faith in the possibility and efficacy of knowledge, (4) Industriousness, (5) Concentration, (6) Patience, and finally, (7) Realism and practical outlook. Below we shall examine Russell's views on each of the above-mentioned characteristics.

1. Curiosity. According to Russell, curiosity is the corner-stone of child's education. If only the child is bursting with curiosity, which every normal child displays, he can be moulded into channels which not only make education smooth and easy but also lay foundation of all other virtues.

2. Open-mindedness. A curious child is automatically open-minded. He spontaneously welcomes new impressions and does not cultivate fixed opinion. He subconsciously understands that one can learn only as long as inner fire of curiosity burns unabated and does not permit congealing of opinions and beliefs. An open-minded person is a supple and sensitive being whereas a close-minded is like stagnant pool which starts stinking.

3. Knowledge is Accessible. An attitude of utter scepticism makes one cynical and reject any use or purpose of knowing as nothing can be known with any permanency or ever as a workable framework. In order to know, one must fervently believe that knowledge is within human grasp and that blind faith blocks the knowing process.

4. Industry. According to Bertrand Russell, all excellence is both rare and arduous. One must be prepared to make suitable sacrifice to know, that is, work hard and persevere in gaining knowledge. Knowing is not an amusement. It needs labour and ardent work.

5. Concentration. A wayward mind is unable to attain any systematic knowledge. Unless one is able to give one-pointed attention to any subject and his mind flits from one subject to the other, education leads nowhere. It merely dissipates one's vitality. Unless we go into the very depth of the subject-matter and fully grasp what we read or listen, education is fruitless. One must be able to give one's full attention to the subject-matter he is studying; otherwise frustration will be the end result of the knowing. In one word, in the absence of concentration, the education is meaningless and sheer waste of effort. According to Bertrand Russell, knowledge is not an amusement or fun play. It requires depth and seriousness.

6. Patience. As you cannot race against time, you can master anything only after a long spell of effort. Anxiety and hurry, as the old saying goes, make curry, an amorphous something lacking any substance. Hence, patience is an essential virtue of a true learner.

7. Realism. A practical attitude towards education is that one should make continuous and relentless effort. This non-stop effort can produce ennui and dispiritedness; but nothing worthwhile is achieved without stubbornness and an ability to put up with routine. A scientist may have to wait for years in his laboratory before he gains anything worthwhile. It will be unwise and imprudent to expect quick results. A realistic attitude towards the whole gamut of learning is a *sine qua non* of success.

Though Russell emphasizes that learning should seem easy and an amusement, but an expectation of cheap thrills must be eliminated from one's mind. Education must be accompanied by a sense of duty and dedication.

Before Bertrand Russell, there were two continental philosophers, namely, German August Wilhelm Friedrich Froebel (1782-1852) who founded child-centered educational system of Kindergarten and an Italian educationist Maria Montessori (1870-1952) who developed an educational system based upon spontaneity. Agreeing with the viewpoints of these thinkers, Russell believed that the teacher should act the role of guide and friend to pupils and radiate affection and sympathy for them and should under no circumstances overawe them because of his superior position vis-à-vis child. The teachers should have the same attitude toward all their pupils. They should not be discriminative in their behaviour in class as well as outside. Most importantly, the education should be spontaneous and effortless. This is possible only if the curriculum accords with the genuine interests and preferences of children. The whole process of education must be free from any compulsion or coercion. If the child is made to learn though fear and authoritarianism, he will soon grow weary and impervious to learning. If any child fails to learn his lessons, the reason for this must be objectively assessed. No child should be coerced to learn what is beyond his mental range. If there is any genuine deficiency in the native intelligence of a child and the workload is beyond his capacity, he can be clubbed with other mentally retarded children and given a specialized training. The judicious use of praise and blame is permissible in the educational set-up as visualized by Russell.

The teacher, according to Russell, should gradually expose children to certain fundamentals and encourage them to develop an interest in deep and sustained thinking so that they are saved from shrewd manipulators of moral, religious and political bigotry.

NURSERY SCHOOL

It is a universal truth that children have to grow into adults and assume responsibility of noble citizens and a noble father. The impressions imprinted in the early formative years become the solid framework which may be desirable or undesirable. Therefore, it is of utmost importance that we should devote our child's education.

Now the pertinent question is who should assume the responsibility of developing fine traits, habits and character of child's early years, because if the child learns self-discipline early it will be worthwhile; otherwise he may grow into a whimsical, cynical and ant-isocial adult. Should this trust be entrusted to parents or technically skilled school teachers? According to Russell this function ought to be performed by Nursery school.

A doubt is liable to rise in the mind of some people as to why the parents are deemed unqualified to guide the child properly and instil in him useful habits of self-control, hard work and a capacity to be happy and enjoy life. The reason for this is not far to seek. In our times, the sciences of human behaviour like psychology, sociology and medical sciences have made tremendous stride. We know today much more about human nature than ever before. The impact of impressions imprinted in early life upon later life is now scientifically established. We know much more precisely about nature and the relative role of heredity and environment. To-day, we have an organised systematic knowledge of the science of human behaviour. But barring race cases, the majority of parents lack expertise in these matters. They may love their children and also wish them well but they may lack leisure or knowledge to enable them to look after the needs of their children in a rational manner. Therefore, it is ideal to entrust the development of children in the hands of those persons who are professional, well-trained and have the expertise to guide children. Most of the parents, for example, would humour their unhappy child by providing chocolate, ice-cream, etc. But an unhappy child has a disturbed digestion and if in our desire to make him happy we feed him rich food he would become physically ill besides being emotionally upset. We need an expert who has adequate knowledge of human psychology, health and disease to handle the child objectively and knowledgeably. Therefore, we need to have Nursery schools manned by well-trained teachers who possess specialized knowledge of the various dimensions of child psychology.

According to Bertrand Russell, irrespective of the financial and intellectual status of parents, a child must be trained in a Nursery school under expert supervision, if he is to develop the essential virtues of compassion, an ability to cooperatc, an integral personality and a liberal outlook on life. The deprived parents, of ,cannot provide their children a congenial atmosphere to develop healthy character and rational outlook. But even affluent parents, though capable of providing excellent atmosphere by giving them private gyms, playgrounds and well qualified teachers, make their children arrogant, domineering and sadistic in nature. Such human beings may have been accommodated in feudal society but they will be misfit in a democratic society. And if we want to promote democracy we cannot afford to have people with callous selfishness and authoritarian outlook and character. Therefore, it is essential to have Nursery schools to save the society from the scourge of authoritarianism and citizens who make for war on account of their acquisitiveness, greed and cut-throat approach to life.

Though we have come a long way in our understanding of human nature, the relative role of hereditary and environmental factors in making up of human personality, we do not as yet possess adequate material for what we deem to be proper education. According to Russell, our approach toward fundamental issues must of necessity be pragmatic, and in this context, there are few assumptions which must be accepted. First of all, we must accept that democracy is the best available political and social option. This means that politically, democratic constitutional government is best suited to human civilization and its progress. The rule of law must prevail. Socially speaking, the true ideal of Liberty, Equality and Fraternity implies that our social organization must be based upon the principle of non-discrimination, that is, we must free ourselves from the clutches of caste, creed and religion. All people must be equal and must receive an equitable treatment. Lastly, we must promote secularism and scientific temper. If we wish to promote commonweal and contribute to human happiness, we must so train our children that they do not become victim of any form of bigotry, superstition and duplicity. They must be fearless and at the same time should not terrorize anyone. They must be compassionate and non-acquisitive; they must avoid personal aggrandizement and become self-respecting individuals who neither overlord over anyone nor succumb to undue pressure.

For the above-mentioned purpose, education must be universal and begin quite early in life. According to Bertrand Russell, a child above two years age must be exposed to social influences; he must start learning to live together and co-operate. If we pamper our children or let them live according to their whims, we shall obstruct the growth of healthy cohesive society and children will grow into resentful and violent adults. This will produce social chaos and wars would be inevitable. In the western world there are many educational institutions based on Froebel and Montessori models. However, quality education is available only to privileged few. According to Russell, this is highly undesirable and unless education is made available to all classes of individuals, irrespective of their financial status, society will remain in turmoil and social violence would spread. If we want peace and progress, education must receive top priority in the society and the greatest attention should be paid to Nursery education. For this purpose, we must have able and dedicated educators who are fired by some inner compulsion to better the lot of mankind rather than seek it as a means of livelihood. Unless best brains come forward voluntarily and in the spirit of social service to teach very young, we cannot but expect social chaos.

CURRICULUM FOR LESS THAN 14 YEARS OLD

The life of man can be divided in segments like childhood, adolescence, adulthood and old age. Each stage of man's life has its own peculiar characteristics and needs. Keeping these two dimensions in view, a person should be assigned those tasks whose level of complexities is appropriate to the level of awareness. Only then we can expect a student perform these task successfully. For example, if children are exposed to abstract discipline they would simply be at sea and would feel frustrated instead of deriving any kind of benefit. Therefore, we have to be careful about what can be taught to children. The very young have to learn whatever is possible by handling toys and minimum exposure to learning of alphabets, counting and writing letters of alphabets. Besides there are individual differences which cannot be ignored. Some have uncanny ability with numbers while others can be made to learn nothing beyond simplest sums. But they may evince keen interest in music, drawing and painting. Moreover, the subjects differ in level of abstraction. Initially we should expose children to concrete subject matter like geography, history, civic and science and gradually introduce subjects of varying abstractions. According to Russell, mathematics should not be introduced earlier than seventh year and even here arithmetical geometry should precede algebra which is of advanced level in abstraction. However, up to the age of fourteen, the education should be broad-based. It should be general and elementary and no specialization should be introduced till this age. Up to the age of fourteen, children should be exposed to all subjects which are useful in the conduct of life. For example, every child should know world geography with the help of charts, globes, maps and as much visual material as possible. The world history should be taught. But it should be uniform in all countries and free from all parochialism. Modern histories are calculated to fan patriotism and nationalism and therefore emphasize the virtue of one's own country and the disparagement of others. This produces biased and fanatical adults who consider other people wicked and undeserving of our sympathy; rather cruelty to them is perceived as justified. Up to the age of five, a child should know reading and writing and doing of elementary sum. They should also learn to dance and sing.

Drawing and painting and music should be taught but intellectual pursuits involving abstraction should not be introduced earlier than the age of seven. Till the age of seven, children should be taught with the help of audio-visual aids and should only learn what can be geographically explained. Russell believes that an International Commission of historians should be established to rewrite history in the world perspective emphasizing the art, culture and the role of common people rather than eulogizing military heroes, warrior kings and rapacious politicians who unleashed wars and consequent misery on common man. While an objective record should be given, an effort to explain its disastrous impact of war upon common people who are uprooted from their countries and have had to bear untold misery should be graphically explained so that from the very early years children should develop a strong antipathy for war and violence and when they grow they will be able to resist whipping of nationalist frenzy leading to internecine killing. According to Russell, if the human energy expended on war is canalized into constructive channels, the scourge of poverty, deprivation, malnutrition, disease and perpetual fear psychosis can be wiped off the face of earth. The main thrust of

Russell's social and educational philosophy is to convince mankind that war is not only not inevitable but it is at the root of human misery. A perpetual sense of insecurity in mankind is a single factor which fans each and every negative emotion in men. If this fear is permanently removed, for happiness will be attainable from almost all people. The happy man, Russell vehemently believes, is a good man. This is the main reason for Russell's passionate commitment to education because it is the only tangible means to transform the outlook of man for positivity and creativity. A proper course of history, Russell believes, will kindle the imagination of child and help him become an optimist. According to Russell, children should be told about the progress of man from a hunter to an agriculturist and subsequently become a master of his destiny by controlling the elements by his cultivation of capacity to think, reason and plan. All this should be brought home to child by the interesting story of Promethen's discovery of fire and the life of great adventurers like Columbus, Vasco da Gama and innovators like Leonardo da vinci and great savants like Lord Buddha, Jesus Christ, Hazarat Mohammed, Solomon, Mahatma Gandhi, etc.

Russell is a staunch supporter of introducing children to collective dance and drama as these not only refine their aesthetic perception but also help keep them healthy by exercises involved in dance. Modern aerobics are a form of bodily dance. Besides dance, children should be exposed to noble literature and poetry and encouraged to express themselves by composing poems and stories. However, the exposure should not be indiscriminate. The literature which may excite violent emotions has to be avoided. Like Plato Russell favours censorship in this regard. Aesop's fables and stories of Panchatantra are the kind of literature suitable for small children. As regards languages, Russell favours teaching of modern languages which are of practical value and frowns upon compulsory education of ancient Greek and Latin. Before introducing algebra, the child should be made familiar with geometry. Russell agrees that mathematics is not everyone's cup of tea and therefore, disfavours its compulsory study barring elementary skills of computation which are essential for a useful life.

EDUCATION FOR 14 TO 18 YEARS OF AGE

The education beyond 14 years of age should be reserved for only those who possess adequate talent and can benefit from it. Everyone need not be compelled to study beyond matriculation.

The subjects which are suited for higher education can be classified as follows :

1. Classical Languages and Literature;
2. Mathematics and Science and
3. Humanities.

The students should be given specialized education in accordance with their aptitude and talents. Before a student launches upon any specialized subject, he should know everything about it in detail and should be allowed to evaluate for himself what suits him. As for Physics, Chemistry and Mathematics, Russell does not subscribe to the usual primacy accorded to Mathematics because Mathematics is regarded queen of sciences. But according to Russell, a great Physicist and chemist need not be a great mathematician as well and viceversa. Russell is a realist and he knows from personal experience all the intricacies involved in scientific pursuit. Therefore, he is not in favour of thrusting upon anyone a subject for which he has no special talent. A mere belief in the exalted status of mathematics does not justify its forced learning, particularly if one can become a great scientist without any specialization in mathematics. However, as regards life sciences, Russell favours compulsory education in anatomy and physiology because if we have adequate comprehension of the structure of our body and its functions, this can help us in maintaining our health.

As regards classical languages, Russell is opposed to the compulsory teaching as was prevalent in his times. According to him, knowledge of German and French can be more useful than Latin and Greek. Those who have special talent for these languages are most welcome to study these subjects. At this stage of learning, the pupil should not be a passive listener. The education of this level should be participative. The education must be a dialogue. Besides, there must be facilities of excellent libraries and laboratories. The students should be allowed to read widely and deeply, but at the same time they should prepare notes from whatever they study. They should prepare essays and show them to teachers so that a teacher may know what is most interesting to a pupil. This would facilitate further guidance on proper lines.

As regards humanities, the study of Philosophy, Economics and Politics forms a group which those interested may study. Russell's first and foremost emphasis in education is that it should wipe out orthodoxy, traditionalism and fanaticism and encourage the scientific temper. It must be clearly appreciated that whatever the value of mysticism and spiritual, the rule of reason and logic can be circumvented at one's own peril. Those who break logic are broken by logic.

DAY SCHOOL *VERSUS* BOARDING SCHOOL

There is a controversy among educationists regarding the relative merits of Day School and Boarding School. The choice between Boarding Schools will of course be determined by circumstances and preference of parents. There is no doubt that new schools can be built away from the hustle and bustle and madding crowd of cities. They can be built upon, funds permitting, on spacious places having lush green playgrounds, vast libraries, swimming-pools and a race course for horse-riding. They can have amphitheatre and assembly halls besides well maintained and furnished classrooms along with a state-of-the-art hostel accommodation. Here the diet and exercise of children can be strictly monitored. The healthy nutritious food under the supervision of dietitians and best cooks can be provided. Besides, as teachers would also be staying in the campus itself, an energetic intellectual atmosphere would prevail. If such ideal schools are available, the obvious choice will be a Boarding school. Moreover, city-dwellers are on the average living in rather congested quarters which are not good for the intellectual, moral and physical health of children. When a child finds his friends spending time in library or debating, his intellectual growth is stimulated. Not many parents are very judicious in giving or holding their love and affection to children. They either pamper the child or neglect him. Both cases are harmful to the child. Therefore, Boarding schools are a better bet for most of the children. However, when a child is highly introvert and physically in poor health, he is likely to feel adverse impact of comparison and competition which is inevitable in Boarding schools. Such children need special care which can be best provided at tome. Moreover, if some new ideas have to be tried or if some new experiment is to be launched, its results can be best monitored if all students share common circumstances and this is best possible in a Boarding school.

However, while there are numerous advantages of Boarding school, there is a flip-side as well. Firstly, the ideal Boarding schools are too few and competent teachers still less. The exclusive schools are preserve of super-rich and the children studying there are liable to become arrogant, class-conscious and status quoists. They will hardly help amelioration of the misery of the world. They would develop vested interests to perpetuate it. Therefore, unless the possibility of wars is eliminated and whopping defence budgets whittled down drastically and monies released used for investment into education, the conditions ideal for human democratic society cannot be created. To have small oases in the vast desert of the educational field is indeed harmful. Instead of being islands of excellence and virtue, they will be schools for making of dictators, overlords and megalomaniacs.

In view of the above discussion, the Day schools have at least the merit of providing tender care and affection of family members. To feel that one is wanted, cared and loved is the *sine qua non* of sane and rational human beings. Those who bear the scars of neglect and indifference in early life are sure to grow into callous-hearted persons. The boarders also live in an artificial world and when they return to society they suffer from superiority complex. They are unable to adjust with hard realities of the actual world. Hence they usually fail to carry on successfully the profession of their families. Moreover, they lack the capacity for mutual respect and honest friendship. But day scholars learn these good qualities by living amidst family members.

As discussed above there are merits and demerits in Boarding as well as Day schools. The choice depends upon circumstances and attitudes.

UNIVERSITY EDUCATION

Russell believes in a highly selective university education. Every child who has graduated from school is not capable of higher education. Only a select few can be benefited from university education. The university education requires high intellectual skills and a capacity for sustained and abstract thinking. Unlike vocational education, the university education is primarily theoretical in content.

Usually the children of privileged classes seek university education. This is not because they need it but merely because they can afford it. The admission of students of lesser calibre leads to over-all degeneration of higher education. Witness the maximum use of secondary reading materials by the students of Indian universities. Throughout their education career they may not read even a single original work. The use of primary material in university education is becoming less and less. This is worrisome. The university educational is not for mediocres; only students with above average intelligence can profit from it. Therefore admission to universities should be given through rigorous competition. Excellence, according to Russell, is both rare and difficult. This means that a university student should be highly intelligent as well as diligent. He should have a sense of dedication and be prepared to work very hard.

The universities have the dual role of producing professionals as well as researchers. University education is a prolonged affair because thorough mastery of any subject requires much time and hardwork coupled with a long period of research. Only very rich or gifted people can afford it. In order to overcome this difficulty there should be many educational trusts and research foundations.

Over and above all these things, a university needs highly gifted and competent teachers. They should be zealously devoted to the pursuit of education and should serve as role models.

According to Russell, after every seven years, a teacher should get a sabbatical year which should be devoted to studying and working in some foreign countries.

A university teacher should devote his time equally in the preparation of his lectures and doing research. There is an explosion of knowledge in the modern world and in order to keep abreast of latest developments, the teacher should have a well equipped personal library besides having free access to all libraries of the world.

A university, according to Russell, must be universal in its outlook and approach. It should not be a means of promoting a particular set of beliefs or ideologies. Indeed, people of varying or even diametrically opposite persuasion should be allowed to work in full freedom. No body should be debarred from university on account of religion, belief or creed.

9

JOHN DEWEY

(1859-1952)

John Dewey, greatest of the pragmatists and generally recognized as the most outstanding philosopher America has yet produced, made significant contributions to virtually every field of philosophy as well as to such other areas of inquiry as education and psychology. Active for seventy years as a scholar, he was a prolific writer publishing approximately fifty books and more than eight hundred articles. Many of these have been translated into various foreign languages. New volumes are still coming out with more Dewey material, mainly correspondence and books and articles on him are appearing at a rapidly increasing rate.

Some Dewey material is at present available only in Chinese. In February and March of 1919 he lectured at the Imperial University of Tokyo, and these lectures were published as *Reconstruction in Philosophy*. While is Japan he was invited to lecture in China also, and he spent from May 1, 1919 to July 1921 there, finding the development there of extremely great interest. He lectured extensively in Peking, Nanking and Shanghai, speaking in English from brief lecture notes; and his lectures were translated and recorded in full on the spot in Chinese by his former students. Dr. Hu Shih's account in *John Dewey in China* Dewey provided the translators and recorders with his typed lecture notes in advance of each lecture so that they could study them and think out suitable Chinese words and phrases before the lecture and its translation. The translation was checked against his notes before publication in newspapers and periodicals or later publication in book form what was known as *Dewey's Five Major Series of Lectures in Peking*, some fifty-eight lectures on Modern Tendencies in Education, Social and Political Philosophy of Education, Ethics and Types of Thinking, according to Hu Shih, went through ten large reprintings in book form before Dewey left China, and continued to be printed for at least three decades before government authorities on the mainland put a stop to them. There were also series on such other topics as Democratic Developments in America, Experimental Logic, History of Philosophy, and (as an introduction to Russell's lectures there in 1920) Three Philosophers of Modern Period, James, Bergson and Russell.

Fortunately, the Institute for Advanced Projects East-West Centre, University of Hawaii, with Professor Robert W. Clopton as special consultant, has undertaken to translate these materials, and in the fall of 1964 Dr. Tsuin-Chen Ou began the work of translation as the first of a team of translators. When this material is available it may well shed significant new light on various areas of Dewey's thought.

The Southern Illinois University Co-operative Research Project on Dewey publications has discovered a number of previously unlisted publications by Dewey, and it has assembled the most complete collection in existence of works by and about him. Under the direction of its Editorial Board, Professors George E. Axtelle, Je Ann Boydston Joe H. Burnett (University of Illinois), S. Morris, Eames and Lewis E. Hahn, the project with the cooperation of a number of other leading Dewey scholars, is planning a definitive edition in forty or more volumes of all his published writings (books and articles). The materials are to be arranged chronologically with careful textual editing but with a minimum of interpretive comment. The editorial and textual work connected with this pioneering venture for a major American philosopher had to extend over many years, but it was hoped that the first volumes will be ready from the Southern Illinois University Press in 1967. Accompanying the works was to be a one-volume Reader's Guide with interpretive essays by eminent Dewey scholars on the main subject areas of his thought and writings. It was expected that this volume will be completed by 1967 so that it may be used throughout the publication period of the works.

Further evidence of the contemporary relevance of Dewey, especially in education, broadly conceived, may be had in connection with the activities of the John Dewey Society for the Study of the Education and Culture. Organised at Atlantic City in February, 1935, it exists to promote the study of the educational aims and educated methods of a democratic society. Regular meetings are scheduled in connection with the annual meetings of the National Society of College Teachers of Education. Much of the work of the Society is carried on through its commissions on Meetings and Communications, Monographs in Educational Theory, and Annual John Dewey Lectures. It helped launched the journal, *Educational Theory*, and it has had a distinguished series of year-books going back to 1937 when William H. Kilpatrick edited the first on *The Teacher and Society*. Among the other editors for this series were Harold D. Alberty, Christian O. Arndt, George E. Axtelle, Harold Benjamin, Theodore Brameld, Bovel H. Bode, John S. Brubacher, Samuel Everett, Hollis L. Caswell, H. Gordon, Hulfish, Virgil Clift, Archibald Anderson, Ernest O. Melby, Harold Rugg, William Van Til, Harold G. Shane, Lindly J. Stiles and William W. Wattenberg. The Annual Dewey Lectures have included Ordway Tead, Oscar Handlin, Seymour Harris and Gardner. Arthur G. Wirth is the current Chairman of the Society's Commission on Publications.

John Dewey's Thought

For one who has written so voluminously and who has made major contributions in so many different areas, no brief summary can be fully adequate. Selecting a few emphases, moreover, is especially dangerous in connection with the thought of one who commonly transcended conventional categories and boundaries and who habitually saw special topics in terms of larger contexts.

And yet if one is to discuss this complex thinker as well as a group of others in a single chapter, a high degree of selectivity is required. It can only be hoped that many readers will be led to turn to extensive reading in his works to supplement these remarks.

1. Reflective Inquiry. Perhaps the most important single emphasis of John Dewey is his insistence upon applying reflective or critical inquiry to problems or indeterminate situations. What is involved in problem solving or thinking through a problem? What is critical inquiry? How does one apply intelligence to human affairs? Dewey's answer to these questions is set forth in its simplest terms in *How to Think*; and a more sophisticated version is given in *Logic : The Theory of Inquiry.* In a sense, the phases or steps in a complete act of reflective thinking afford an outline for each of his major works; and he had a life-long concern with what is involved in reflective thinking.

(i) The first step in a complete act of reflective thinking is the appearance of the problem. This may be marked by a more or less vague sense of something having gone wrong, a breakdown in habitual responses or modes of action. One of our beliefs is questioned or acting upon it leads to a conflict or perplexity.

(ii) The second step or phase is clarification of the problem. Through analysis and observations we gather sufficient data to formulate the difficulty or define the problem. If, for example, a belief is disrupted, questioning or analysis may indicate what precisely is in dispute.

(iii) With problem clearly stated we pass to the stage of appearance of suggested solutions or hypotheses as to how to solve the problem. Various ideas occur to us as to how it may be solved.

(iv) The fourth stage is that of deductive elaboration. We reason out the implications of the various hypotheses. If we take the first hypothesis, we may expect such and such consequences; or need to make additional observations or gather more information to see what may be expected. If we take the second one, we may expect such and such other consequences; and so on. On the basis of a survey of the implications of the various proposed solutions we decide which to test in action.

(v) The fifth step is that of verification. Through observation or experiment we check out the hypothesis or hypotheses which looked most promising to us. If one of the hypotheses works out, the indeterminate situation is replaced by a determinate one in which stable lines of action are possible; instead of the problematic situations or perplexity we have a resolved or clarified one.

These steps or stages do not necessarily come one right after another in the sequence in which these have been listed here. For example, the first three stages may be telescoped in such a fashion that we do not get clear indication of the stages, but in general, the more difficult the problem, the more likely the stages are to be clearly outlined before it is solved. Or, again, after we have reached the stage of deductive elaboration, we may discover that we need to go back and further clarify the problem or think of additional ways of trying to solve it.

Though this pattern is somewhat oversimplified, in fundamentals this is basically accurate. This is what is involved in problem solving activity whether it is a personal problem, an important social conflict, or a weighty scientific problem. When we solve a problem in this way, moreover, we have not merely a solution to our difficulty but also some descriptive or explanatory statements about how it was solved.

2. Experience. Experience is one of the central concepts in Dewey's thought, occurring and recurring throughout his writing. Though he finally concluded that he might have done better to use another term, many of his most important works are concerned with clarifying it, for example, his *Carus Lectures*, *Experience and Nature*, or his *Art as Experience* or *Experience and Education*. For him experience constitutes the entire range of men's relations to or transactions with the universe. We experience nature and things interacting in certain ways make up experience.

For a brief presentation Dewey's views can perhaps best be summarized in terms of a contrast with what he calls the orthodox view of experience, that is accepted by both the traditional empiricists and their opponents. Whereas the orthodox view treats experience primarily as a knowledge affair, Dewey speaks of it as intercourse between a living being and its physical and social environment. The traditionalists regard as subjective inner affair, separate and distinct from objective reality; but Dewey has always thought of experience as being of a piece with the objective world, which enters into the actions and sufferings of man and which, in turn, may be modified through human response. Instead of a gulf between disparate inner and outer realms of being, one may move freely from experience to that which surrounds, supports, and maintains it. The proponents of the orthodox view have been preoccupied with what is 'given' in a bare present, whereas Dewey was more concerned with what might be done to change what is given or taken, in furtherance of human purposes. The older empiricists thought in terms of what has been or is given, looking toward the past if they passed beyond the present. For Dewey the salient trait of experience is its connection with a future. If change is what we are interested in, we look primarily towards the future, and not recollection but anticipation is central for the experiment form of experience.

One of the main differences between Dewey's and the orthodox view of experience, however, turns about the latter's particularism, its concern with sense data to the neglect of connections and continuities, and its supposition that relations and continuities are either foreign to experience or are dubious by-products of it. Dewey, like James, emphasized the relations. The contextual, situational, transactional or field character of experience stands out in his account. The traditional view opposed experience and thought in the sense of inference, but for Dewey experience is full of inference, as might be expected for one who sees the directional and relational character of experience. Where one seeks to control what is to come through employing present environmental supports to effect change which would not otherwise occur, inference is of vital importance. From the standpoint of the future life activity of the organism, environmental incidents are favourable or hostile; and if one is to eliminate the latter and insure the former, an imaginative forecast of the future is essential for guidance in this process.

The structure of experience, however, comes out most clearly on Dewey's view of aesthetic experience. There we have experience in full, vivified, clarified, and intensified.

3. Knowledge. Dewey rejects the traditional epistemology which sets up a knower outside the world and then asks about the possibility, extent and validity of knowledge in general. He laughingly suggests that we might equally well have a problem of digestion in general — its possibility, extent and genuineness — by assuming that the stomach and the food-materials were inhabitants of different world. The significant problem is not how such a knower is somehow to mirror the antecedently real out but rather one how one set of experienced events is to be used is signs of what we shall experience under another set of conditions. The important distinction, moreover, is not between the knower as subject and the world known as object. Instead it is between different ways of being in the movement of things, between an unreflective physical way and a purposive intelligent one.

On Dewey's view knowledge needs to be placed in the context of the problematic or indeterminate situation and reflective inquiry. Knowledge is more than immediate awareness or the presence of a set of sense data. Having qualities before us does not constitute knowing. Knowledge is always inferential, and the problem is how the processes of inference are to be guided to trustworthy or warranted conclusions. It involves operations of controlled observation, testing and experimentation. It is a product of inquiry — the stems in a complete act of reflective thinking. Dewey liked Bacon's idea that knowledge is power and it may be tested by the promotion of social progress.

4. Philosophy. In *The Need for a Recovery of Philosophy* Dewey declared that philosophy must cease to be "a device for dealing with the problems of philosophy" and become "a method, cultivated by philosophers, for dealing with the problems of men." But the problems of men as he sees them cover a range broad enough to include in one way or another most of the traditional problems as well as many others. The method involves treating philosophy as vision, imagination and reflection; and though the clarifying process may show that certain epistemological problems are pseudo-problems, the fact that they are raised may point to genuine cultural crises. If action at all levels needs to be informed with vision, imagination and reflection to bring clearly to mind future possibilities with reference to attaining the better and averting the worse, there is more than enough for philosophy to do.

Developing an adequate conception of the place of intelligence in human affairs is one important task for philosophy. How can intelligence which is a creation of a culture also be a creator or forming influence on that culture? How can it define the larger patterns of continuity between past and an insistent future? How can philosophy adjust the body of traditional beliefs to scientific tendencies and political aspirations which are novel and incompatible? These are tasks which involve the application of reflective inquiry on the broadest scale possible, and in applying it we need to remember what Dewey reminds us in the little essay on *Philosophy and Civilization*, that in philosophy we are occupied with meaning rather than truth. This, of course, is not to deny either the crucial importance of truths as subclass of meanings or the relevance of existence to meanings. It is rather to suggest that imaginative sweep, values and significance are our primary concern.

In *Reconstruction in Philosophy* Dewey stresses the social function of philosophy, holding there that the task of philosophy is to clarify men's minds as to the social and moral issues of their day, to enlighten the moral forces which move mankind, and to contribute to the aspirations of men to attain a more ordered and intelligent happiness.

For Dewey, in general, philosophy is both a product of human culture and a process of criticizing or clarifying it, distinguishing meanings within and helping to give it direction and form. In *Experience and Nature* he speaks of philosophy as criticism of criticism; as the "critical operation and function become aware of itself and its implications." It becomes a kind of theory of criticism — a consideration of alternative ways of critically evaluating values and beliefs.

5. Meaning, Values and Beliefs. Meaning and values are focal in Dewey's conception of philosophy, and this aspect is not lost when he treats philosophy as general theory of criticism. For him we criticise for the sake of instituting and perpetuating more enduring and extensive values; and each of the various philosophical disciplines, metaphysics no less than the others, makes its distinctive contribution to this end.

6. Biologism. What is sometimes referred to as Dewey's biologism reflects (a) his emphasis on the genetic point of view and (b) his conviction that inquiry has a biological matrix. He was interested in how ideas originate and become more complex, in the parallels between human responses and lower levels, and in the continuity of different species of organic life from the lowest forms to man. To understand the present situation, he held, we inquire into its specific condition as well as into its probable consequences.

Darwin and James helped Dewey to see the focal importance of the living creature adjusting or adapting to its environment and to view intelligence as a distinctive form of behaviour — one concerned with choosing appropriate means for the attainment of future ends. Whatever else mind may be, it is at least a means of controlling the environment in relation to the ends of the life process. Within this framework, the senses are not primarily gateways to knowledge but signals to redirect action, or signs of problems to be solved. In *The Influence of Darwin on Philosophy* Dewey suggests that the philosophic lesson of Darwin is that philosophy itself becomes a method of locating and interpreting the most serious of the conflicts that occur in life and a method of projecting ways of dealing with them.

7. Experimentalism. Dewey's experimentalism relates to his analysis of reflective inquiry for which hypotheses, prediction and experimentation are central. An experiment is a programme of action to determine consequence. It is a way of introducing intelligence into a solution. It is an intelligently guided procedure for discovering what adjustments an organism must make to its environment to ward off evil or to secure goods. Experimentation for Dewey is relevant not merely on the individual biological level, but wherever planned reconstruction of a situation may help effect desired transformation, for example, in social planning or in education. The more important are the issues at stake, the more clearly is experimentation seen to be preferable to such alternatives as authoritarianism, simple guesswork or merely waiting for events to run their course.

In some ways the best contrast with Dewey's experimentalism is the *Quest for Certainty*. Whereas Descartes sought demonstrable proof or certainty through reason and Berkey took sensory awareness as the bedrock of certainty, Dewey argued that what we are really after is not certainty of any sort but security in the face of a hostile environment. We are trying to stablise responses or adjust successfully to a hostile environment.

8. Instrumentalism. Dewey's instrumentalism also stems from his analysis of reflective inquiry. Ideas are not copies, images or visions of external objects but rather tools or instruments to facilitate an organism's behaviour. They are instruments for operating on things or on stimuli. Things or objects are what we can do with them, and we can distinguish among them by the behaviour reactions they make possible.

Truth, accordingly, is adverbial. It is a way ideas work out in practice. It is a matter of whether hypotheses lead to predicted consequences, an affair of verified predictions warranted assertions.

Dewey's instrumentalism encourages a new respect for instruments, or means. The more we value ends or goals, in his view, the greater is our attention to the means which may bring them about. The separation of goods into natural and moral or into instrumental and intrinsic may have the harmful consequence of making moral and intrinsic goods more remote from daily living besides encouraging us to think that we can have the intrinsic without having to concern ourselves with the instrumental. Viewing any good as merely instrumental, moreover, is fairly sure not to do it justice.

9. Relativism. Dewey's relativism is to be opposed to absolutism and is a way of stressing the importance of context, situation, relationships. To take things out of relations is to deprive them of value and meaning. Absolutes are ruled out in his view and unqualified generalizations are likely to be misleading. An economic policy or a plan of action is a good relative to a specifice situation which makes it desirable. A knife may be good for sharpening pencil and bad for cutting a rope; but to speak of it without qualification as good or bad is quite misleading.

10. Meliorism. In ethics, according to Dewey's account in *Reconstruction in Philosophy*, the emphasis should be placed on improving or bettering our present situation rather than upon good or bad in some absolute sense. The good if one is to speak of the good rather than the better, is what will enable us to solve the problem or difficulty. Thus, what is usually referred to as a moral end or standard becomes in his view a hypothesis as to how to overcome a moral problem. Since every problematic situation is unique, values are unique; but if one is to specify an end, then growth, education, or problem solving, would be that end. Instead of treating acquisition of skill and attainment of culture as ends, we should see them marks of growth and means to its continuing difficulties or furthering growth.

In the *Quest for Certainty*, Dewey's Gifford Lecture, we find a somewhat different approach, stressing the construction of the good; and in this construction, it is argued, we have to test our likings, enjoyments and desires; we do this by checking on the conditions and the results of certain forms of enjoyment or liking, and this involves running through the steps in a complete act of reflective thinking. It is not simply a question of whether as a matter of fact we do not enjoy or like something but whether this enjoyment or liking meets the test of reflection. It is not merely enjoyed or desired but also desirable or enjoyable in the sense of being worthy of being desired or enjoyed. When we say that something is desirable we are claiming that future consequences will be such as to meet the test of reflection.

Further discussion of Dewey's views on valuation and some of the questions growing out of his view may be found in the *Theory of Valuation* and in Ray Lepley, Editor, *Value : A Co-operative Inquiry* in which Dewey, H.D. Aiken, C.E. Ayaes, A.C. Garnett, G.R. Geiger, L.E. Hahn, B.E. Jessup, H.N. Lee, Ray Lepley, E.T. Meichell, Charles Morris, D.H. Parker, S.C. Pepper, and P.B. Rice re-examine fundamental issue of value.

11. Humanism. Dewey's humanism stems from his acceptance of the Beconian view that knowledge is tested by promotion of human intelligence based in good part on the experience of modern science for the sake of bettering the human situation. Supernaturalism and the usual dogmas of revealed religion have no place in Dewey's view. As he tells us in *A Common Faith,* the things of greatest value in civilization exist by the grace of the continuous human community in which we are a link, and we have the responsibility of conserving, transmitting, rectifying and expanding our heritage of values in order that those who come after us may share it more generously and more securely. Our common faith draws its main stand from our attempt to carry out this responsibility.

Dewey's humanism is expressed also in his democratic outlook. As he saw it, democracy as a way of life is controlled by a working faith in the possibilities of human nature. Granted proper condition, and Dewey devoted a lifetime to working for them, human intelligence can work out aims and methods by which experience can grow in richness. His faith in discussion, persuasion, education and conference techniques, as opposed to force or coercion as a way of resolving differences was at one with his democracy or his faith in human nature. With free inquiry, free assembly and free communication of ideas, the convinced, reflective inquiry is self-corrective.

12. Art as Experience. On Dewey's view, as set forth in *Art as Experience*, there is an aesthetic quality in all experience and not merely in works of art. His account stresses the continuity between everyday experience and art. Wherever experience is vivified, clarified, intensified and unified, we have an aesthetic experience more meaningfully, more coherently, and with greater vividness, clarity and intensity, than daily life ordinarily manifests. The humdrum and the routine are the chief enemies of the aesthetic. Ordinarily, we simply recognize objects for this use, but if we can have full perception of them, take in their full quality for its own sake, then we have an experience in a distinctive sense.

If any experience has the potentiality of becoming something appreciated for its own quality, then, human intelligence has the responsibility of applying aesthetic principles, not merely in art, but to our houses, our machine products, our cities, our highways, and our general environments.

PHILOSOPHY OF EDUCATION

Most of the major theses in Dewey's general philosophy find expression in his philosophy of education. Reflective inquiry is as central for education, in his view, as for any other phases of life of experience. Indeed, for him, education is a problem-solving process and we learn by doing, by having an opportunity to react in real life situation. In education, not in doctrination, inquiry is focal. Not simply amassing facts but learning to apply intelligence to problem-solving has top priority. Education must be experimental without being simply improvisation.

The reconstructive purpose is as much at work in education as anywhere else in experience. As Dewey put in *Democracy and Education*, "Education is a constant recognizing and reconstructioning of experience." Present experiences must be so guided as to make future experience more meaningful and worthwhile. Though the values and the knowledge of the past are transmitted, they must be done in such a fashion as to broaden, deepen and otherwise improve them. Criticism and not simply passive acceptance is demanded.

Dewey equated education and growth. As teachers we start with the child where he now is, with his present stock of interests and knowledge and seek to help him expand and enrich both his interests and his knowledge and grow as a person in his community and his society. He learns to work responsibly for his own development and for social conditions which will encourage a similar development of all other members of his society. Education must not be simply a means to something else. It should not be merely preparation for the future. As a process of growth it should have its own enjoyable and intrinsically rewarding features at the same time that it helps further continued education and, in Dewey's view, the test of our social institutions may be found in their effect in furthering continued education on growth.

Dewey himself had considerable reservations over some features of progressive education, but he continued to emphasize some of the strengths of the newer education as compared with the traditional outlook. His humanism and meliorism are richly exemplified in his account of the theory and practice of education. His philosophy of education stresses the social nature of education, its intimate and multiple relations to democracy and its cultural significance.

AIMS OF EDUCATION

1. Development. According to Dewey, the aim of education is the development of child's powers and abilities. It is impossible to lay down any definite principle for a particular kind of development, because this development will differ from one child to the next, in conformity with the unique abilities of the individual. The educator should guide the child according to the abilities and powers he observes in it. It is better in Dewey's opinion to leave the question of educational objectives unanswered. If a definite aim is ascribed to education, it may do great harm by compelling the teacher to guide the educand in a particular direction, not in keeping with the innate abilities of the child. In general, the aim of education is to create an atmosphere in which the child gets an opportunity to be active in and contribute to the social awakening of the human race. From the pragmatic standpoint, education aims at creating social efficiency in the child. Man is a social being who must develop within the confines of society, outside which he cannot develop at all. For this reason, education must aim at creating social efficiency and skill.

2. Creating Democratic Individual and Society. Pragmatic education aims at instilling democratic values and ideals in the individual, at creating a democratic society in which there is no distinction between one individual and another. Each individual is completely independent and willing to cooperate with others. Every individual must be given the freedom to develop his own desires and achieve his ambitions. Every individual must be equal to every other members of society. Such a society can be created only when there is no fundamental difference between the individual and collective interests. Hence education should create cooperation and harmony among individuals of democratic society in which the child undergoes various forms of development, of which moral education and development are the most important. Morality can be developed through active participation, because such participation in the activities of the schools trains the child in shouldering responsibility. This develops the individual's character and gives him social skill. Equality of opportunity in the school helps to develop boys and girls according to their own individual interests and inclinations.

3. Preparation for Future Life. Pragmatic education is basically practical in as mush as it aims at preparing the individual for future life in such a manner that he can fulfil his requirements and achieve contentment. Future life in the pragmatic sense implies not merely individual life but also social life. Deway was critical of the contemporary modes of education because they tend to drive the child away from democratic life by giving advantages to a small section of society. It also lays more stress on book or formal teaching than is really desirable. This mode of teaching compels the educand to listen to long lectures which blunt his own mental powers. Hence, Dewey laid the foundations of a progressive education in the form of a Progressive School which aimed at establishing democratic values and developing the child's personality.

CURRICULUM

Dewey believed that the educational process has two aspects, psychological and social.

1. Psychological. The curriculum and the method of education should be determined by the child's instincts and abilities. The child should be educated according to his interests and inclinations. Education should be attempted only after discovering the interests of the child, and these should be used as the basis for determining the curricula for the various stages of education.

2. Social. All education has its beginning in the individual's participation in the social consciousness of the race. Hence, it is necessary to create an atmosphere in the school which will allow the child to take an active part in the social awakening of his group. This improves his conduct and develops his personality and abilities.

Principles of Curriculum

Dewey has stressed the following four principles as underlying the formation of educational curriculum.

1. Utility. The curriculum imposed on the child must have some utility meaning thereby that the curriculum should be based on child's interests and inclinations during various stages of his development. In general, the child evinces four major interests — the desire to talk and exchange ideas, discovery, creation and artistic expression. The curriculum should be conditioned by these four elements and designed to include the teaching of reading and writing, counting manual skill, science, music and other arts. It is not desirable to introduce the child to all these subjects at once, but to teach a subject only when it is desired at a particular stage of mental development.

2. Flexibility. It is better for the curriculum to be flexible and not predetermined and rigid. It must be capable of accommodating the changes in the child's interests and inclinations.

3. Experimental. The curriculum should be related to the child's contemporary experiences and these can be multiplied and reinforced by presenting different kinds of activities in the guise of problems which inspire the child to attempt solution. In this way, the variety of his experience can be increased. As far as possible, the teaching of each subject should be related to the content of child's experiences.

4. Close to Life. As far as a possible, the curriculum should include only those subjects which can be related to the child's pattern of life at that particular stage. This proximity to life can help in creating a distinctive unity in the knowledge imparted to him, and thereby some harmony can be created in the teaching of history, geography, mathematics, language, etc. Dewey was very critical of the contemporary method of dividing knowledge into separate compartments, because he felt that such fragmentation of knowledge was unnatural. As far as possible the various subjects in the curriculum should be harmonized.

EDUCATIONAL METHOD

1. Learning by Doing. Dewey, himself a successful educational psychologist, has presented many novel and useful ideas on educational methods in his two books, *How We Think* and *Interest and Efforts in Education*. The most well-known principle enunciated by him is the theory of learning by doing in which the child learns best when he himself performs actions related to particular subjects. The educator is not to stuff the child's mind with information he himself has gathered throughout his life, but to guide the child to those activities by which the child can develop his own natural abilities and qualities. The child should be acquainted with facts while he is engaged in activity relating to those facts. Besides, the child should be confronted with practical difficulties and problems which he should try to solve. Problem solving is a good technique because it adds to the child's experience.

2. Integration. Dewey is of the opinion that there should be integration between the child's life, his activities and the subjects he studies. All subjects to be taught to the child should be arranged around his activities in such a manner that he acquires knowledge in the process of doing activities to which he is accustomed. Dewey's principle was later on adopted by Mahatma Gandhi in his plan of basic education.

3. Child Centred. The next question that arises is that of designing the method of teaching according to the child's interests. Dewey considers interests and efforts to be of supreme importance in the process of education. The educator must understand the child's interests before organizing the activities which are useful for the child. Given the opportunity to formulate programmes on their own, children will be able to make programmes according to their own interests. It is better if this effort is free of any fear or compulsion, because only then can the children make a programme independently. Once this is done, all school activity takes on the form of self-willed activity.

This method of education is apparently very suitable in as much as it meets the requirements of education in psychology. But in fact it has one inherent shortcoming that if the education of the child is fashioned exclusively according to the child's natural inclination, he will remain ignorant of many subjects. Besides, even his knowledge of other subjects will remain disorganized. These objections have been accepted by Dewey himself.

4. Project Method. Dewey's ideas on educational methods later on led to the evolution of the project method in which the child was made to indulge in those activities which helped in the development of enthusiasm, self-confidence, self-reliance and originality.

5. Participation in Collective Activities. In democratic educational pattern, the child should be made to participate in collective activity which can help in evolving a cooperative and social spirit.

ROLE OF THE EDUCATOR

Servant of Society

Pragmatic education grants considerable importance to the educator, who is conceived as servant of society. His task is to create in the school an environment which will help in the development of child's social personality and enable the child to become a responsible democratic citizen. Dewey considers the educator to be so important that he goes so far as to call him God's representative on earth.

Democratic Guide

In determining the educator's own behaviour in the school, Dewey accepts democratic principles and educational psychology as suitable guides for shaping the educator's conduct. In order to realize the values of equality and independence in the school, the educator should not treat himself as superior to the children. He must also consciously abstain from imposing his own ideas, interests, views and tendencies on the children. He must confine his own activity to an observation of the child's own natural inclinations and personality traits, to engaging the child in suitable activities. Hence, it is essential for the educator to pay constant attention to the individual differences of the children. If this is done, administration of the school becomes easier. The educator must also try and engage the children in activities which compel them to think and reason out things for themselves.

DISCIPLINE

1. Discipline through socialization. If the child conducts himself on the lines suggested above, discipline in the school becomes easy. Difficulties arise only when discipline takes the form of an external force employed to restrain the child from expressing his natural desires. This is the traditional concept of discipline which was severely criticized by Dewey. He argued that discipline depends not only upon the child's own personality but also upon the social environment in which he is placed. True discipline takes the form of social control and this is evolved when the child engages in collective activity in the school. It is, therefore, desirable to create an atmosphere in the school which encourages the children to live in mutual harmony and cooperation. Discipline and regularity of habit can be induced in children by making them act in consonance with each other in trying to achieve a single objective. This objective may be social, moral, intellectual or purely physical.

2. Self-Discipline through School Programmes. School programmes go a long way in creating the child's character. It is, therefore, better to provide the child with a social environment and a mode which inspire him to self-discipline rather than to subject him to a long lecture. By methods such as these, the child can be turned into a really social being. A peaceful atmosphere is undoubtedly conducive to good and rapid work, but peace is only a means, not an end in itself. The educator's real task is to discourage the children to come into conflict with each other; it is not desirable to scold them and compel them to be peaceful. Self-discipline is a better weapon, and this can be taught through responsibility. When the educator is faced with the responsibility of looking after most of the work of the college or school, he automatically evolves self-discipline.

3. Participation in Social Activities. Participation in social activity is an essential part of educational training in Dewey's opinion. The school itself is a rudimentary form of society. If the child is encouraged to take part in all collective activities in the school, he will also be simultaneously trained for many activities he must perform in social life. Thus, he will also learn to lead a disciplined life as an adult.

CRITICAL EVALUATION

Although Dewey's views on educational principles were enthusiastically received, they were also subjected to criticism on the following grounds :

1. Difficulties of not Accepting Truth to be Permanent. Pragmatic philosophy does not treat truth as permanent and objective. Instead, as Dewey explains, all truth is relative to time and space. No philosophy is always true or correct. It has its utility only in a particular set of circumstances. And utility is the final criterion of truth. In actual practice, Dewey's philosophy is fairly useful, but when his principles are applied to his own theories, the latter also become relative to time and space and thus have only a limited utility. Hence, the principle of pragmatism itself becomes only relatively true because it does not accept truth as something permanent.

2. Materialistic Bias. Pragmatism was born out of reaction to idealism and consequently it manifests a distinctly materialistic bias, in contradiction of the spiritual bias of idealist philosophy. At the same time, Dewey wants to realize democratic ideals of freedom, equality and fraternity through education. But it is difficult to understand how this can be done unless he accepts an idealistic basis for his system of education. If worldly success is the only criterion of truth, few if any people will concern themselves with moral superiority, since the latter has no obvious relationship with material success.

3. Absence of Any Aim of Education. The achievement of democratic ideals through education seems to be implicit in Dewey's educational philosophy because he rarely ascribes particular aim to education in explicit terms. For him, education is life itself, and it is not possible to determine any objective for it. Most scholars disagree with this opinion because they believe that education can progress only when it has some definite aim and objective. There is always some definite purpose in sending the educand to school. And even though a school resembles society in many ways, it has a distinct existence within the larger framework of society. Hence, the aims of education must be defined.

4. Excessive Emphasis upon Individual Differences. Modern educational psychology accepts in principle that the curriculum of education must take into account the individual differences of children and that children must be educated according to their individual and unique interests and inclinations both in respect of curriculum and also of the method of teaching. While in theory this is quite acceptable, any attempts to apply it in practice lead to immediate complications. It is almost, if not completely, impossible to provide a separate educational plan for every individual child in a school. It is for this reason that all schools nowadays provide a uniform pattern of education imparted in the same manner. Besides, the teacher may have to educate the educand in a subject in which the latter is not at all interested. Thus, it is not possible to eliminate many complex and difficult subjects from the curriculum only because the student is not interested in them.

5. Limitations in Learning through Doing. There is no doubt that the child should learn actually doing things, as Dewey suggested, yet the theory has its limitations. Many facts known to an individual are acquired from another person. It is almost impossible for one individual to experience every fact known to him. Thus, the educand should also try to benefit from the experience of his teacher, educator and colleagues. The educator must also supplement the educand's efforts at self-education with guidance and communication of his own experience.

INFLUENCE OF MODERN EDUCATION

Many of Dewey's ideas have had great impact on modern education. Some important facts in this connection are the following.

1. Impact on the Aims of Education. Nowadays, one of the important aims of education is the teaching of democratic values. Dewey insisted on developing social qualities in the child. In modern schools these aims of education have been accepted as valid.

2. Impact on Educational Methods. The greatest impact of Dewey's ideas is seen in the methods of education in more recent times. Dewey suggested that education should be based on the child's own experience and also that the method of teaching should vary according to the interests and inclinations of each individual child. These ideas influenced modern teaching techniques and led to active teaching in the schools.

One such school is the Activity School. The project method is also a result of Dewey's ideas. Even in the other schools, attention is paid to the principles of child psychology which guide the educator in creating an atmosphere suitable for developing social consciousness in the educand.

3. Impact on Curriculum. The impact of Dewey's ideas on the subject of curriculum led to the introduction of manual skill subjects into modern curricula. Special importance is now being attached to various kinds of games, objects, the use of certain tools and implements, etc. In selecting the subjects to be taught, attention is now paid to the individual interests and abilities of the child.

4. Impact on Discipline. As a result of Dewey's theorizing on the subject of discipline, now the educand is entrusted with much of the work done in the school. In this manner the educand is trained in self-control and democratic citizenship. Apart from this, once the educand has to face responsibility, he is compelled to think scientifically and reason out things for himself.

5. Universal Education. Dewey's thinking and ideal also led to faith in universal and compulsory education. Education aims at the development of personality. Hence every individual must be given the opportunity to develop his personality through education. The current stress on the scientific and social tendency owes much to Dewey's influence. He pointed out that education was a social necessity, in that it was not merely preparation for life, but life itself. It aimed at the development of both the individual as well as society. This leads to the comprehensive development of the individual.

10

MARIA MONTESSORI

(1870-1952)

Montessori's House of Childhood was situated in the slums of Rome, a European capital. She established the centre of gravity of her system in the environment. In her *The Secret of Childhood* she affirms, "Our own method of education is characterized by the central importance that we attribute to the question of environment; it is well-known how our pedagogy considers the environment so important as to make it the central point of the whole system."[1]

The Association of Good Building was formed to remove the social evils of the poorest quarters of Rome. Its plan was to acquire tenements, remodel them, put them into a productive condition and administer them in the interests of the occupier.[2] The care of reconstructed tenements was given to the tenants, and they did not abuse their trust. Difficulties, however, arose in regard to young children under shcool age, left to themselves during the day. Unable to appreciate the motives which led their parents to respect the property, their children spent their time defacing the buildings. In order to cure this evil, the Director General of the Roman Association for Good Building planned to gather together in a large room all the little ones between the ages of three and seven belonging to the families living in the tenement. The play and the work of these children were to be carried on under the guidance of a teacher who should have her own apartment in the tenement house.[3] Thus, came to be instituted the House of Childhood — the school within the tenement on 6th January, 1907. The expenses of the new institution were met in accordance with the general self-supporting principle of the reconstruction scheme by the sum that the Association would otherwise have been forced to expend upon redecoration and repairs.

The Montessori Method

The Director General of the Roman Association of Good Building entrusted to Montessori the organisation of the infant schools in the model tenements in Rome towards the end of 1906. She adopted her method of training and previous experience. Having graduated in medicine, she was for a time in charge of the training of mentally defective children. She taught a number of such children to read and write so efficiently that they were able to be presented for examination with normal children of the same age. This phenomenal result she attributed to an improved method. She therefore conjectured that if this method is applied in the training of normal children, it would yield even more surprising results.[4]

To be successful, these methods should obviously be applied in the training of infants. At this period of life, the child has not acquired the coordination of muscular movements necessary to enable him to perform dexterously the ordinary acts of life. His sensory organs are not fully developed, his emotional life is still unstable and his volitional powers are irresolute. About the significance of the pedagogical experiment for which the institution of the House of Childhood afforded the facilities, Montessori wrote, "It represents the results of a series of trials made in the education of young children, with methods already used with deficients."[5]

Principles of Montessori Method

The first principle is to train the pupil to be independent of others in respect of the ordinary practices of life. It necessitates approach to the child mind at a lower level than can be adopted with normal children, an appeal to the senses rather than to the intellect. With physically defective children, it implies training one sense to function vicariously for another. The ultimate reference is to the sense of touch which is regarded as fundamental and primordial. The Montessori system accordingly becomes an 'education by touch.' Montessori maintains that the sense of touch is fundamental. It undergoes great development during the early years of life. If neglected at this age, it loses its susceptibility to training.

The Psychological Method

Montessori's psychological method in education implies that the educative process is adapted to the stage of mental development of the child, and to his interest. It is not wholly subordinate to the necessities of a curriculum or to the teacher's scheme of work. "By education," says Montessori, "must be understood the active help given to the normal expansion of the life of the child."[6] The 'psychological moment' in the educative process comes when the consciousness of a need arises in the child mind. In the Montessori method, "It is necessary then to offer those exercises which correspond to the need of development felt by an organism, and if the child's age has carried him past a certain need, it is never possible to obtain, in its fullness, a development which missed its proper moment."[7] If a child fails to perform a task or to appreciate the truth of a principle, the teacher must not make him conscious of his error by repeating the lesson. She must assume that the task has been presented prematurely. Before again presenting the stimulus, she must await the manifestation of the symptoms which indicate that the need exists.The duration of a process is determined not by the exigencies of an authorised timetable, but by the interval which the child finds requisite to exhaust his interest. Thus, in a Montessori school, one may find a pupil working unremittingly at a self-imposed task for several days on end.

No Prizes

In the Montessori system there are no prizes. The pupil's sense of mastery is his highest reward, "His own self-development is his true and almost his only pleasure."[8] Such correction as is admitted in the Montessori system comes from the material, not from the teacher. "From the 'Children's Houses' the old time teacher who wore herself out maintaining discipline of immobility and wasting her breath in loud and continual discourse, had disappeared and the didactic material which contains within itself the control of errors is substituted, making auto-education possible to each child."[9] It is an intellectual discipline by consequences.

Perfect Freedom

The psychological method implies the perfect freedom of the child which consists in absolute obedience to the laws of the development of his own nature. According to Montessori, "The method of observation (that is the psychological method) is established upon one fundamental base — the liberty of the pupils in their spontaneous manifestation."[10] This liberty necessitates independence of action on the part of the child. "Whoever joins a well kept school is struck by the discipline of the children. There are forty little beings from three to seven years old, each one intent on his own work; one is going through one of the exercises for the senses, one is doing an arithmetical exercise, one is handling the letters, one is drawing, one is fastening and unfastening the pieces of cloth on one of the wooden frames, still another is dusting. Some are seated at the tables, some on rugs on the floor."[11]

Adapted Environment

As instruction should be adapted to the stage of development of the pupil, Montessori advocates that the environment should likewise be so adapted. She wrote, "Give the child an environment in which everything is constituted in proportion to himself and let him live therein. Thus, will develop within the child that 'active life,' which has caused so many to marvel because they see in it not only a simple exercise performed with pleasure but also the revelation of a spiritual life."[12] Such an environment should contain the means of auto-education.[13] "He who speaks of liberty in the schools, ought at the same time to exhibit objects — approximating to a scientific apparatus which will make such liberty possible."[14]

Practices of Montessori Method

The practices of the Montessori Method fall into three classes : (1) the exercises of practical life; (2) the exercises in sensory training; and (3) the didactic exercises.

1. The Exercises in Practical Life. Freedom, according to Montessori, does not consist in having others at one's command to perform the ordinary services, but in being able to do these for oneself, in being independent of others. Thus, in the House of Childhood the pupils learn how to wash their hands, using little wash-stands with small pitchers and basins, how to clean their nails, brush their teeth and so on. Exercises are also arranged to train the child in the movements necessary in dressing and undressing. The apparatus for these exercises consists of wooden frames, mounted with two pieces of cloth or leather, which are fastened by means of buttons and buttonholes, hooks and eyes, eyelets and lacings or automatic fasteners. After some practice, in fastening and unloosening the pieces of cloth with various types of fasteners, the child finds that he has acquired a dexterity which enables him to dress and undress himself. Not content with the satisfaction derived from such independence, his consciousness of the possession of a new power excites in him a desire to assist in dressing the whole family.[15] All the furniture in the House of Childhood, tables, chairs, etc. are of such a size and construct that the pupils can handle them easily, they learn to move them deftly and without noise, and are thus afforded a training in motor adjustment.

Montessori devised certain forms of gymnastic exercises to develop coordinated movements in the child. She disapproved of the child practising the ordinary gymnastic exercises arranged for the adult. She maintained, "We are wrong, if we consider little children from their physical point of view as little men. They have, instead, characteristics and proportions that are entirely special to their age."[16] A new set of exercises has been evolved in accordance with general Montessori principles, by observing the spontaneous movements of the child. One piece of apparatus is the little round stair. It is wooden spiral stairway enclosed on one side by a balustrade on which the children can rest their hands. The other side being left open, enables the children to habituate themselves to ascending and descending stairs without holding on. It teaches them to move up and down with poised and self-controlled movements. The steps are very low and shallow. The children can thereby learn movements which they cannot execute properly in climbing ordinary stairways in their homes, where the proportions are suited to adults. The new exercises give the pupils of the House of Childhood a gracefulness of carriage which distinguishes them from other children.

2. Exercises on Sense Training. For the methods and the apparatus of her scheme of sensory training, Montessori is largely indebted to the tests and apparatus employed by the experimental psychologists. However, Montessori is not interested in measuring the powers but in furthering their development. Practice-effects frequently disclose themselves in the application of tests by psychologists, especially when the investigation extends over a long period. These are disturbing factors to the psychologist which he must estimate. However, it is just these practice-effects that sensory education strives to secure.

"To make the process one of self-education," Montessori explains in *The Advanced Montessori Method*, "it is not enough that the stimulus should call forth activity, it must also direct it. The child should not only persist for a long time an exercise; He must persist without making mistakes. All the physical or intrinsic qualities of the objects should be determined, not only by the immediate reaction of attention they provoke in the child, but also by their possession of this fundamental characteristic, the control of error, that is to say, the power of evoking the effective collaboration of the highest activities (comparison, judgment)."[17]

In sensory training Montessori believes in isolating the senses whenever that is possible. This procedure is suggested by the education of physically deficient children. The pupils of the Montessori schools are blindfolded, a feature of the training which seems to add zest to their efforts. The auditory exercises are given in an environment not only of silence, but even of darkness.

The material used in the sensory training recalls the apparatus of the psychological laboratory. For perception of size, series of wooden cylinders varying in height only, in diameter only or in both dimensions at once, are employed. Likewise are blocks varying regularly in size and rods of regularly graded lengths, for perception of form, geometrical insets in metal, in wood or the shapes of the insets drawn on paper; for discrimination in weight; tablets of wood similar in size but differing in weight; for touch, a highly polished surface and sand-paper surfaced; for sense of temperature small metal bowls with caps; for auditory acuity, cylindrical sound boxes containing different substances; for the colour sense, graded series of coloured wools.

Similar methods are adopted in developing in the child tactual acuity, and in training him to discriminate differences in temperature and in weight. In these exercises the child is blindfolded or is enjoined to keep his eyes closed during the tests; he is encouraged to do so by being told that he will thus be able to feel the differences better.

The exercises which are directed to the development of form play such an important part in the Montessori system as to entitle them to separate treatment. The first exercise is to sort out of a heap of bricks and cubes such as are the forms of these merely by grasping them; they do not require to trace the contour. This exercise may be varied by the use of different materials, as for example, by the use of coins, and so expert do the children become that they can distinguish between small forms which differ but little from one another, such as corn, wheat and rice.

The real training in the perception of form begins, however, when the child passes to the exercises of placing wooden shapes in spaces made to receive them, or in superimposing such shapes on outlines of similar form.

Geometric insets of various designs, the initial ones strongly constrasted, the later ones merely dissimilar forms of the same figure, as for example, the triangle, are mixed up and have to be sorted out by the children and fitted into the frames made to receive them. The frames furnish the control to test the accuracy of the work. Montessori method is determined purely from the pedagogical standpoint, and that the objects most commonly met with in practical life, table tops, doors, window frames, etc. are of this form.

In learning to fit the geometric insets into the spaces provided for them, the child employs not only the visual sense but also the tactual and muscular senses. He is taught to run the index finger of the right hand around the contour of the form and to repeat this with the contour of the frame into which the inset fits. It is frequently observed that children who cannot recognise a shape by looking at it do so by touching it. According to Montessori, "The association of the musclar-tactile sense with that of vision, aids in a most remarkable way the perception of the forms and fixes them in memory."

From the exercises with the solid insets in which the control is absolute, the child passes to exercises in the purely visual perception of form. The wooden insets have to be superimposed on figures cut out of blue paper and mounted on cards. In a further series of exercises, the figures are represented by an outline of blue paper, which for the child represents the path which he has so often followed with his finger. Finally, he is required to superimpose the wooden piece on figure whose outlines are represented merely by a line. He thus, passes from the concrete to what is relatively abstract, from solid objects to plane figures represented merely by lines and perceived only visually.

Through such exercises, the forms of the various figure circles, ellipses, triangles, rectangles, etc. come to be known. When the need for them becomes urgent, the names of the figures are given. As no analysis of the forms is undertaken, no mention is made of sides and angles; the teaching of geometry is not being attempted at this stage.

3. The Didactic Exercises. The methods adopted in training the perception of form prepare the way for the teaching of writing and of the other didactic processes.

Popular interest was aroused in the Montessori method by the success attending the application of the didactic processes of writing, reading and numbers. At the inception of the system it was not intended that such exercises should be included. Therefore the results were incidental.

TEACHING OF WRITING

In the Montessori system the teaching of writing precedes the teaching of reading. Montessori maintained that in normal children the muscular sense is most easily developed in infancy and this makes the acquisition of writing exceedingly easy for children. In writing to dictation, the child translates sounds into material signs and performs certain movements, the latter process being easy and usually affording pleasure to the child.

In accordance with her general principle, Montessori adopts psychological standpoint in respect of writing. "Let us observe an individual who is writing and let us seek to analyse the acts he performs," she proposes, and again, "It goes without saying that we should examine the individual who writes, not the writing, the subject, not the object."

According to the Montessori view, writing is not a mere copying of headlines, but the writing of words which express ideas. In writing are involved two diverse types of movement, the movement by which the forms of letters are reproduced and that by which the instrument of writing is manipulated. In addition, the phonetic analysis of spoken words into their elementary sounds is also necessary. Preparatory exercises for each of these factors must be devised and practised independently before writing is actually commenced.

As the children had already learned to know the forms of the geometric insets by running their fingers round the contour, so, to teach the forms of the letters, Montessori tried to get the pupils to trace with the finger the shapes of the letters cut out in sandpaper and pasted on cards, the roughness of the sandpaper providing a control for the accuracy of the movements. As soon as they have acquired facility in this tracing of the forms of the letters, the children take great pleasure in repeating the movement with closed eyes. Thus the forms of the letter are not learned and impressed on the minds of the pupils by visual analysis and retained by visual imagery, but by tactual and motor experience and grapho-motor imagery.

The phonetic sounds or the letters are taught at the same time as the tracing of the forms, the steps in the lesson following the three-stage procedure already illustrated. The audio-motor imagery helps to reinforce the grapho-motor and to facilitate the retention of the forms of the letters. The children are also practised in analysing the spoken word into its sounds and in reconstructing the word with sandpaper letters.

The control of the pen is also attacked indirectly. Recourse is for this training to the geometric insets, of which mention has already been made. Taking one of the metal frames into which the inset fits, the child draws on a sheet of paper with a coloured crayon around the contour of the empty frame. Within the figure which results he places the metal inset, and with a crayon of a different colour traces the outline of the inset. Thus are reproduced the two figures in different colours upon the paper. With another crayon of his own selection, the pupil fills in the figures which he has outlined. In making the upward and downward strokes he is taught not to pass outside the contour. Variety is lent to the task by the choice of different coloured crayons and by the use of different insets, the employment of the letter also training him to make upward and downward strokes of various lengths. Gradually, the lines tend less and less to go outside the enclosing boundary until at last they are perfectly contained within it. Both the centre and the frame are filled in with close and uniform strokes. The child is now master of the writing instrument; the muscular mechanism necessary to its manipulation is established.

Now the three prerequisites to writing are at the pupil's command, that is, he has acquired control of the writing instrument, he can reproduce the forms of the letters moving his figures in the air, and the composition of words out of the isolated sounds of letters can be effected psychically. At this point the imitative tendency in the child arouses in him the impulse to write. Now a pupil who has given no previous indication of having developed ability in this direction begins to write straightway.

TEACHING OF READING

The way to the teaching of reading is prepared in the Montessori system by the procedure adopted in the teaching of writing. In the exercises preparatory to writing is included word-building with sandpaper script characters representing the sounds of the spoken word. Reading demands the inverse process, that is, the reproduction of the sounds from the symbols and the fusion of these sounds into words. The proper accentuation of the syllables is also necessary for the correct enunciation of the word. This comes only with recognition of the meaning. Montessori refused to give the name 'reading' to anything less than this. Just as writing is something more than mere copying pothooks and headlines, so reading is not a mere 'barking at print' but the recognition of the meanings represented by the visual characters. She says, "What I understand by reading are signs." "Until the child reads a transmission of ideas from the written words he does not read."

The didactic material for the lessons in reading consists of slips of paper or of cards upon which are written words and phrase in clear large script.

The lesson begins with the reading of names of objects which are known or which are present. The child is given a card on which a name is written in script. He translates the writing slowly into sounds. If the interpretation is exact, the directress restricts herself to saying 'Faster.' The child reads more quickly the second time, but still often without understanding. The teacher repeats, 'Faster, Faster.' The child reads 'Faster' each time repeating the same accumulation of sounds. Finally, the word emerges in consciousness. When the child has pronounced the word, he places the card under the object whose name it bears, and the exercise is finished. It is a lesson which proceeds very rapidly since it is only presented to a child who is already prepared through writing.

Sentences describing actions or expressing commands are likewise written on slips of paper. The children select these and carry out the requests contained in them.The child does not read the sentences aloud.[18] The aim of reading is to teach the child to discover ideas in symbols, hence the reading should be silent and not vocal. According to Montessori's analysis, reading aloud implies the exercise of two mechanical forms of language — articulate and graphic — and is a complex task. The child, therefore, who begins to read by interpreting thought should read mentally. "Truly," claims Montessori, "we have buried the tedious and stupid ABC primer side by side with useless copy-books."[19]

The period intervening between the commencement of the writing process and the appearance of the ability to read is about a fortnight. Facility in reading is, however, arrived at much more slowly than in writing. Normal children trained according to the Montessori method begin to write at four years of age and at five know how to read.

TEACHING OF NUMBER

In the teaching of number in the Montessori system is used the 'long stair,' a set of ten rods, the first being one metre in length, the last one decimetre, the intermediate rods diminishing in length by decimetres. The rods are divided into decimetre parts, the space on the rods being painted alternately red and blue. When arranged in order they form what is called the 'long stair.' They are utilized in the sensory exercise for training the children in discrimination of length. In these exercises the rods are mixed up, and the teacher grades them in order of length, calling the child's attention to the fact that the stair thus constructed is uniform in colour at one end. The child is then permitted to build it for himself.

After the child has had practice in arranging the rods in order of length, he is required to count the red and the blue divisions, beginning with the shortest rod, thus: one, one, two, one, two, three; always going back to one in the counting of each rod and starting from the same end. He is then required to name the various rods from the shortest to the longest, according to the total number of divisions each contains, at the same time touching the rods on the side on which 'the stair' ascends. The rods may then be called 'piece number one,' 'piece number two,' and so on, and finally, they may be spoken of in the lessons as one, two, three.

The graphic signs for the number are cut in sandpaper, and by the three-period lesson arrangement previously illustrated the pupil is taught to associate the names of the numbers with their graphic forms. The graphic signs are then related to the quantity represented.

TEACHING OF ARITHMETIC

Addition may then be taught by suggesting to the child to put the shorter rods together in such a way as to form tens : 1 is added to 9, 2 to 8 and so on. Substraction, multiplication and division can also be introduced by means of didactic material, and later on the child is allowed to express graphically his operations with the rods.

The means and methods of dealing with the larger denominations of number and the higher arithmetical processes are dealt with in *The Advanced Montessori Method* and also deal with the teaching of drawing, music, grammar and prosody.

RECAPITULATION PRINCIPLE

Montessori accepts the recapitulation principle in education, "The child follows the natural way of development of the human race. In short, such education makes the evolution of the individual harmonise with that of humanity."[20] In *The Advanced Montessori Method,* however, Montessori rejects the recapitulation principle discussing it as "a materialistic idea now discredited."[21]

ROLE OF THE TEACHER

The Montessori method works through the employment of teachers possessed of a training in child-psychology and in its application to young children. According to Montessori, "The broader the teacher's scientific culture and practices in experimental psychology, the sooner will come for her the marvel of unfolding life, and her interest in it."[22] "The more fully the teacher is acquainted with the method of experimental psychology, the better will she understand how to give a lesson."[23] The training of the teacher should enable her to refrain from intervening. According to Montessori, "In the manner of this intervention lies the personal art of the educator."[24] Montessori has substituted the term 'directress' for the title 'teacher.' She has to acquire the power of silence. Instead of teaching, she has to observe; instead of the proud dignity of one who claims to be infallible, she assumes the gesture of humility.[25]

REFERENCES

1. M. Montessori, *The Secret of Childhood* translated and edited by Barbara B. Carter (London : Longman's Green & Co., 1936), p. 137.
2. M Montessori, *The Montessori Method,* p. 56.
3. *Ibid.,* p. 43.
4. M. Montessori, *The Advanced Montessori Method* translated by Florence Simmonds and Lily Hutchinson (London : William Heinemann, 1917), Vol. i, ch. 3.
5. *Ibid.,* p. 45.
6. *Ibid.,* p. 104.
7. *Ibid.,* p. 358.
8. *Ibid.,* p. 356.
9. *Ibid.,* p. 371.
10. *Ibid.,* p. 80.
11. *Ibid.,* p. 346.
12. *Ibid.,* p. 72.

13. *Ibid.*, p. 72.
14. *Ibid.*, pp. 19-20.
15. Josephine Tozier, *An Educational Wonder-Worker : The Method of Maria Montessori* (New York : The House of Childhood Inc., 1912).
16. *Ibid.*, pp. 139-40.
17. *Op. cit.*, p. 75.
18. *Ibid.*, p. 301.
19. *Ibid.*, p. 298.
20. *Ibid.*, p. 160.
21. *Ibid.*, p. 255.
22. *Ibid.*, p. 89.
23. *Ibid.*, p. 107.
24. *Ibid.*, p. 176.
25. *Ibid.*, p. 128.

11

HERBERT SPENCER

(1820-1903)

Spencer, an eminent thinker who made singular contribution to educational philosophy, was born in 1820 in Derby (U.K.). His father was a confirmed rationalist and a free thinker who believed that the child should be encouraged to develop his talents through self-effort; any attempt to force any pattern or system upon him would stultify his native genius. By profession he was a school-teacher who had known from personal experience that the freedom to grow is essential for a child. The external influences inhibit natural talent and that all artificial attempts to inculcate education are counter-productive.

Early in his life Spencer was trained in Physics, Chemistry and Geometry. His father exposed him to some other discipline as well and by the age of seventeen he had learned enough for his age.

In 1838, Spencer took keen interest in mechanical subjects and wanted to become a civil engineer. But he made certain technical innovations and engaged himself in business. However, as a businessman, he met with little success and turned away from it and became interested in literature. In 1848 he became an Associate Editor of *The Economist.* It was here that he came in contact with eminent personalities like George Elliot, Julian Huxley and Mathew Tundal.

In 1858 he gave up the work of editing and journalism and flowered into full-fledged wholetime writer. In the year 1855 he published his first book *The Principles of Psychology* and in 1858 he started a quarterly *A System of Philosophy*. Subsequently, he wrote numerous important books like *Education* (1861), *First Principles* (1862), *The Principles of Biology* (1864-67), *The Principles of Ethics* (1892-93), *The Principles of Sociology* (1876-96), *Essays* (1857-74), *Various Fragments* (1897), *Facts and Comments* (1902) and *Autobiography* (1904). In 1896 he lived at Brighton and died here in 1903.

THE AIMS OF EDUCATION

Spencer was not a traditionalist. Like his father he was a free thinker and open to new ideas. He believed that the child was quite capable of self-effort and education. He could develop his talents and attitudes without external pressure or guidance. He must be provided a milieu which did not frustrate his native talents. It should pave way for his untrammelled growth and full flowering of his personality. Spencer was critical of the prevalent curriculum. According to him, it did not emphasize adequately the practical aspect of child's personality; it did not equip the child with abilities to cope effectively with the exigencies of his adult life. The education should enable a child to lead to a successful and fruitful life. The test of good education is its ability to enable a man to live fruitfully and productively. The child should know how to develop himself physically and mentally for a self-fulfilling happy life. He should be capable of self-management and capable of independent decisions. Besides, he should be able to upkeep his family, become a noble citizen capable of making effective use of natural and social resources. As natural sciences equip the child to become a useful citizen, the study of these sciences should be emphasized.

FIVE TYPES OF HUMAN ACTIVITIES

Herbert Spencer has divided human activities into five divisions :

(1) Self-preservation activities;

(2) Indirect self-preservation activities;

(3) Procreational and parental activities;
(4) Activities directed towards becoming and developing intelligent, political and civic life and
(5) Leisure and recreational activities.

According to Herbert Spencer, by studying various sciences one can perform all the above-mentioned tasks efficiently. Hereunder we shall study the sciences relative to each type of activities.

(1) Self-Preservation. Nature, according to Spencer, takes care of all our needs of self-preservation. However, nature takes care of our preservation only as long as we ourselves do not frustrate or inhibit our sponteneous and natural activities. Toward this end Spencer stresses the need to study thoroughly Anatomy, Physiology, Physics and Chemistry. Spencer is confident that a thorough knowledge of the subjects would ensure sound health.

(2) Indirect Self-Preservation. The indirect self-preservative activities are those which are conducive to accomplishment of self-preservation purpose. Spencer cannot visualize a purpose which cannot be successfully achieved by the scientific techniques. The needs of food, clothing and shelter can be met by sciences of agriculture, textile and architecture. The sciences of Geology, Mathematics, Chemistry and Astronomy affect human life in one way or the other. Spencer recommends a thorough study of these sciences.

(3) Rearing of Children. Herbert Spencer is in favour of imparting parenting and child caring education at the school level itself. An average parent is innocent of the techniques of child rearing. Therefore, school children should be trained in child caring so that they can grow into wise parents.

(4) Citizenship. Spencer wants that educational curriculum should be such as to make children become noble citizens. Toward this end the knowledge of History is essential. Herbert Spencer was not satisfied with historic literature of his times. According to him History should not be opinionated and subjective. It must be objective and this can be done only by imbibing the spirit of science in writing of books on History. He urged redrawing of the books on History so as to make historic records comprehensive and objective.

(5) Leisure. Herbert Spencer's outlook on life was very liberal. He fully recognised the vital need of leisure and recreation in life. For this he recommended production of creative writing, literature and art. He wanted children to learn drawing, painting, music and sculpture. However, he was of the opinion that the study of sciences should precede humanistic disciplines; even art and culture should be, according to Spencer, rooted in science. For example, a sculptor will be in a great advantage and make excellent statues if he possesses the knowledge of anatomy and mechanics. According to Spencer, a medical expert will write superior poetry though this is obviously a curious view. Due to his overwhelming passion for science, Spencer remained innocent of the spiritual values and he could not appreciate adequately the value of humanistic studies. But it must be admitted that in laying greater stress on science in education Spencer was ahead of his time.

THEORY OF EDUCATION

Herbert Spencer has propounded some outstanding principles of education. But it must be admitted that these lack originality. Indeed he has only synthesized the ideas of his predecessors. However, he has put them in a systematic order and it is for this innovative sum-up that we are indebted to him. Hereunder we describe them in the form of easily comprehensible formulas.

1. From Simple to Complex. This principle of educational theory is commonsense. In order to understand a complex event or fact we must begin with simple facts which are easily comprehensible to a child. Once the simple facts are fully grasped it is easy to understand the complex because what is complex is but a chain or permutation and combination of simple facts. By this means child can be made to understand complicated events and facts. This is a principle which is of first and foremost significance in education.

2. From Known to Unknown. This principle is nothing but a most simple to complex route sensible in education. Nothing unknown can be recognized, much less understood. But if the same set of facts is put in a way with which we are familiar, it can be safely presumed that simple facts will enable us to understand the complex. A teacher should explain the complex situation establishing them as logical conclusion for simple and well understood facts.

3. From Indefinite to Definite. To begin with, the children have vague knowledge, but as they grew in age and become mature their grasp of complex facts comes by them automatically and their ideas become transparent and definite. For example, the sun, moon and planets are mere isolated facts but when we learn various facts holistically we have more definite knowledge. This truth is a psychological axiom and every intelligent teacher uses it sponteneously. Spencer has merely restated it.

4. Education through Entertainment. According to Spencer if we tap the native interests of children we can assimilate our knowledge structure in them so that a child does not experience knowing a load but a pleasant exercise. The education should be creative and become a source of joy to the child. If we tell children what is somehow related to their likes and aptitudes they will willingly grasp at it and want to know more and more in the line. We all know how children love to hear stories and these narratives can enlighten as well as entertain.

MORAL EDUCATION

Spencer is on the whole critical of current parental attitude toward children. It is more of an expression of vanity of elders. They pretend to teach children what they practise more in breach than in performance. In order to inculcate love of moral life Spencer wants radical restructuring of family ties. The morality should be developed through precepts rather than empty locations.

Spencer wants the parents to so formulate the moral principles that these are in tune with the Nature. As any violation of nature carries a corresponding punishment so should violations of moral principles have in-built punishments. As misuse of fire burns, water drowns or gives some other physical discomfort, similarly breach of moral principles should become automatically hurtful. For example, dishonesty and lying belittle one in the eyes of one's peers and lose face. A liar gets automatic rebuff, so should be with all those acts which are morally suspect.

Spencer is opposed to corporal punishment. For example, if a child steals he should not be beaten but his pocket expenses stopped for an appropriate period. If a child dirties his clothes deliberately he should be asked to clean these up by washing with soap, etc. Spencer is opposed to any cruelty towards children. They should be treated kindly and with a smile. They should be encouraged to become self-dependent.

Spencer is advocate of according full freedom to children and they should be allowed to develop it by self-effort and control. There should be no coercion and no undue discipline. Nothing should be done to hurt the child. However, while excessive discipline is really uncalled for and application of force to correct the behaviour of children is undesirable, it cannot be denied that a certain amount of discipline is essential and that the child has to be trained to do things which are basically unpleasant. A modicum of unpleasantness is unavoidable if excessive libertarianism is to be checked which is fundamentally against the true interests of the child.

PHYSICAL EDUCATION

Spencer favours a scientific attitude to physical exercise. He points out four defects in the current physical curriculum :

(1) Children are not given a balanced diet;

(2) They do not get adequate clothes;

(3) They are not allowed adequate physical exercise and

(4) They are intellectually overtaxed.

Spencer was a progressive educationist and he has done well to emphasize the need of physical exercise.

EVALUATION

Spencer has critically influenced modern educational system by laying a wholesome emphasis upon intellectual, moral and physical education. He has rightly emphasized the primacy of scientific education and a respect for the freedom of the child.

Many philosophers are critical of Spencer's views upon education because he has purportedly neglected the spiritual aspect of education and laid an exclusive emphasis upon materialistic development of human personality. But it must be said to the credit of Spencer that he has helped democratization of education and freed it from exclusive confines and priviledges of aristocracy.

Spencer's views were, moreover, very much in tune with the contemporary philosophy of education. He recognised that everyone could not receive encyclopaedic education. Each person has certain potential and peculiar talent. Each should be allowed to get whatever and as much education as he is capable of. Any force-feeding of educational material would be counter-productive.

Secondly, Spencer is criticized for regarding education as a preparation for life. He over-rates the value of education. But this fault is common to all those thinkers who over-emphasize scientific education. In fact, education is a part and parcel of life and it is wrong to alienate it from life.

As regards the methodology of education, Spencer has made no novel suggestion of his own in this respect. He has merely elaborated the methods outlined by Pestalozzi (1746-1827).

Spencer has been roundly criticized on account of his over-emphasis upon science; but it is little realized that the meaning that Spencer attached to science was very broad-based. He includes moral education also in the precincts of science. He wanted schools to become more integrated to life. He wanted to replace classical education by scientific discipline. He considered sciences as the best means of human enlightenment. But he rather neglected the value of language and literature in human life.

12

IGNATIUS LOYOLA

(1491-1556)

The Jesuit Society

Ignatius Loyola, a knight of noble birth, recognised that all available gifts of intellect and birth would be required for the crusade which the Company of Jesus was enrolled to wage. Consequently, it gave him peculiar satisfaction when the tests imposed on candidates for admission to the Society were passed by youths of noble birth. The Society devoted itself mainly to higher education. Its aim was to arrest the disintegrating forces in the religious life of Europe. To effect this it was necessary to attack the evils at their source, namely, in the universities, hence the Society's concern for higher education.

According to the Constitution of the Society, instructing others in reading and writing would be a work of charity if the Society had a sufficient number of persons available, but on account of dearth of teachers it is not ordinarily accustomed to undertake this.

Public Education

The Jesuits extol public education as T. Hughes puts it, "For this moral strengthening of character, no less than for the invigorating of mental energies, the system of Ignatius Loyola prescribes an education which is public — public, as being that of many students together, public as opposed to private tutorism, public, in fine, as requiring a sufficiency of the open, fearless exercise both of practical morality and of religion."[1]

After his surrender to the Christian life, it was early borne in on Loyola, that without proper education his labours would be of no avail whenever thirty years of age resolved to acquire from the beginning the Latin rudiments and patiently to learn his lessons among the ordinary pupils. Bringing to his studies an adult mind of a surprisingly practical type and an unerring judgment, he could reflect upon the methods employed, and from his own initial failures deduced a procedure from which others might profit. Francis Thompson writes, "One knows not whether more to admire his astonishing determination of his astonishing mental power, when it is reflected that he carried through his philosophical studies at the age of forty-four, having begun his whole education from the very elements others acquire in boyhood."[2]

On the 3rd May 1539, a series of resolutions was adopted by the few companions to whom Ignatius Loyola had communicated his ideas of founding a society, agreeing : (1) to take an explicit vow of obedience to the Pope; (2) to teach the Commandments to children or anyone else; (3) to take a fixed time — an hour more or less — to reach the Commandments and Catechism in an orderly way; (4) to give forty days in the year for this work.

The Constitutions

Loyola set forth the fundamental principles of the Society in the *Constitution of the Society.* It consists of ten parts, the fourth and largest of which presents in outline the plan of studies which was later more fully elaborated in the *Ratio Studiorum.* In Part I of the Constitution, Ignatius Loyola prescribed the conditions of admission to the Society. In Part II, he recounts the causes justifying the dismissal of probationers of members of the Order. According to Loyola, the Society should demand of its entrants the qualities which Plato in the *Republic* required of his philosophers. "It is needful," Loyola states, "that those who are admitted to aid the Society in spiritual concerns be furnished with these following gifts of God. As regards their intellect; of sound doctrine, or apt to learn it; of discretion in the management of business or, at least, of capacity and judgment to attain to it. As to memory; of aptitude to perceive, and also to retain their perceptions. As to intentions: that they be studious of all virtue and spiritual perfection; calm, steadfast, strenuous in what they undertake for God's service; burning with zeal for the salvation of souls, and therefore attached to our Institute; which directly tends to aid and dispose the souls of men to the attainment of that ultimate end, from the hand of God, our Creator and Lord. In externals facility of language, so needful in our intercourse with out neighbour, is most desirable, a comely presence, for the education of those with whom we have to deal. Good health, and strength to undergo the labours of our Institute. Age to correspond with what has been said; which in those admitted to probation should exceed the fourteenth year and in those admitted to profession the twenty-fifth. As the external gifts of nobility, wealth, reputation and the like are not sufficient, if others are wanting; so, if there be a sufficiency of others, these are not essential; so far, however, as they tend to edification, they make those more fit for admission, who even without them, would be eligible on account of the qualities before mentioned; in which, the more he excels who desires to be admitted, so much the more fit will he be for this Society, to the glory of God our Lord, and the less he excels, so much the less serveable will he be. But the sacred function of the divine wisdom will instruct those who undertake this duty to His service and more abundant praise, what standard should be maintained in all these things."

Physical Education

In Part III of *The Constitution* a chapter is included 'Of the Superintendence of the Body.' Speaking from his own experience, Loyola frequently warned his companions against the subversive influence of an enfeebled bodily condition. The charge frequently made against the Jesuit system of education, that it does not regard the physical care of the pupil, is accordingly not warranted by the Constitutions of the Society.

Educational Organisation and Management

The aim and scope of thé work of colleges has been thus described, "As the object of the doctrine to be acquired in this Society is by the divine favour to benefit their own and their neighbours' souls, this will be measure in general and in particular cases, by which it shall be determined to what studies our scholars should apply, and how far they should proceed in them. And since, generally speaking, the acquisition of diverse languages, logic, natural and moral philosophy, metaphysics, and theology, both scholastic as well as what is termed 'positive' and the Sacred Scriptures assist that object, they who are sent to our colleges shall give their attention to the study of these faculties; and they shall bestow greater diligence upon those subjects which the supreme Moderator of the studies shall consider most expedient in the Lord to the aforesaid end, the circumstances of times, places, and persons being considered."[3]

Order of Studies

The order of studies to be followed is first the Latin language, then the liberal arts, thereafter scholastic, then positive theology. The sacred scriptures may be taken either at the same time as the foregoing or afterwards.[4]

The Scholars

The scholars shall be assiduous in attending lectures, and diligent in preparing for them; and when they have heard them, in repeating them; in places which they have not understood, making inquiry; in others, where needful, taking notes, to provide for any future defect of memory.[5] Latin was commonly to be spoken by all, but especially by the students in humanity. Since the habit of debating is useful, especially to the students in arts and scholastic theology, instructions are given as to when and how these debates or disputations are to be arranged and conducted. There should be a common library in each college of which the key is to be given to those who ought to have it. Besides these, however, every one should have such other books as are necessary.[6]

Those scholars who intend to devote their lives to the work of the Society are further instructed in the performance of the ordinances of the Church; "and to discharge this duty let them labour to acquire thoroughly the vernacular tongue of the country."[7]

The Universities Curriculum

The universities which the Society shall establish or maintain shall consist of the three faculties; languages, arts and theology;[8] "the study of Medicine and of the Law shall not be engaged in within the Universities of our Society; or at least, the Society shall not take that duty upon itself, as being remote from our Institute."[9] The curriculum in arts shall extend over three and a half years, and that in theology over four years. In the arts curriculum reference is made to the natural sciences which 'dispose the mind to Theology, and contribute to its perfect study and practice, and themselves assist in the same object.' It is further enjoined that the natural sciences, 'be taught by learned professors, and with proper diligence, sincerely seeking the honour and glory of God in all things.'

Modification Possible

Provision was made by Loyola in the Constitutions for modification of his outline plan of studies according to circumstances. This concession should not be abused. The uniformity of the system should not be destroyed. It was considered expedient that an authoritative yet more detailed plan of studies than that outline in the Constitutions should be issued for the guidance of the schools and colleges of the Society.

The Ratio Studiorum was accordingly prepared on the main source of the educational doctrines of the Society. *Jourvancy's Ratio Discendi et Docendi* is regarded as the official complement to, and commentary on, *The Ratio Studiorum.*

Ratio Studiorum

Unlike the *Constitutions, The Ratio Studiorum* deals exclusively with education. It sets forth the following rules and regulations :

1. Which are to direct the Superior of a Province in dealing with Education in his Province.
2. The Regulations which the Rector of a college is to apply in governing a college.
3. The guidance of the Prefect of Studies.
4. General regulations for the professors of the higher faculties — theology and philosophy.
5. Special rules for the professors of each subject in the faculties sacred writings, Hebrew, scholastic theology ecclesiastical history, canonical law and moral or practical theology, moral philosophy, physics and mathematics.
6. Regulations for the Prefects of the Lower studies.
7. Regulations for the conduct of written examinations.
8. The general regulations for the professors of the lower classes.
9. Detailed regulations for the professors of rhetoric, humanity and higher, intermediate and lower grammar.
10. Rules for the pupils for the management of Academies, etc. are added. The Ratio Studiorum comprehends all subjects from the principles governing the educational administration of a province to the fixing of school holidays, the text books to be used in teaching Latin grammar and the method of correcting exercises.

General Organisation of the Educational Work

It may be gathered from the regulations issued for the direction of the curriculum that the theological course of four years is the highest. It is preceded by a course of philosophy extending over three years. The Provincial shall not send pupils to philosophy before they have studied rhetoric for two years. All students in the philosophical course must attend lectures in mathematics. Students who show special proficiency in any subject should have the opportunity of extending their study of that subject. The classes for the Lower Studies are not to exceed five; one for rhetoric, another for humanity and three for grammar. These classes are not to be confused with one another. Parallel classes for the various grades are to be instituted as the number of pupils warrants it.

Regulations for the Rector of a College

The need of trained teachers even for the lowest classes is recognised. The teachers of the lower classes should not take up the work of teaching without training. The Rector of the college should select some one specially skilled in teaching. Towards the end of their studies the future teachers should come to him three times a week for an hour to be trained for their calling in methods of exposition, dictation, writing, correcting and all the duties of a good teacher.

Prefect of Studies

In Colleges the Rector appointed a Prefect of Studies as his assistant. His position was somewhat analogous to that of the Dean of a Faculty. He was responsible to the Rector for the proper organisation of studies and the regulating of classes so that those who attend may make as much advancement as possible in uprightness of life, the arts and doctrine. The Prefect of Lower Studies is ordinarily responsible for both studies and discipline. In boarding schools he exercises both functions within class hours. A Prefect of Studies may have as assistant a Prefect of Discipline whose duties in a boarding schools would be somewhat analogous to those of a Bursar in an English Public School or in a University College.

General Regulations for Professors

The educational aim of the Society is recalled in the General Regulations for all the professors of the higher faculties. It is to lead the pupil to the service and love of God and to the practice of virtue. Each Professor is required to offer up a suitable prayer before beginning his lecture. Directions are given as to how far authorities are to be followed and used by the professors in lecturing, and how are they to lecture that the students may be able to take proper notes. After each lecture the professor is to stay for a quarter of an hour for interrogation by the students about the substance of the lecture. At the end of each session a month is to be devoted to the repetition of the course. The last general rule for all the professors is that the professor is not to show himself more familiar with one student than with another; he is to disregard no one, and to further the studies of the poor equally with the rich; he is to promote the advancement of each individual student.

Detailed directions follow for the professors of each of the subjects in the faculties of theology and philosophy. In the 1832 revision of the Ratio, special provision was made for the teaching of physics, which had previously been treated under the general title philosophy. The regulations for the teaching of mathematics were modernised.

The Rules for the Prefect of the Lower Studies

He is to help the masters and direct them. He is to be especially cautious that the esteem and authority due to them be not impaired in the least. Once a fortnight he is to hear each one teach. He is to see that the teacher covers the class-book in the first half-year and repeats it from the beginning in the second term. Promotion is generally given after the long vacation, where it would appear that a pupil would make better progress in a higher class. He is not to be detained in the lower class but to be promoted at any time of the year after examination. When there is a doubt whether a pupil should ordinarily be promoted, his class record are to be examined, and his age, diligence and the time spent in the class are to be taken into consideration. While intimating promotions the names of the pupils gaining special distinction are to be announced first; the others are to be arranged in alphabetical order. To further the literary training of the pupils the Prefect is to institute Academies or school societies. In these, on specified days, the pupils are to hold lectures, debates, etc. Amongst themselves. A Censor is to be appointed, one who is held in esteem by his fellow-pupils and who shall have the power to impose small penalties. For the sake of those who are wanting in diligence and in good manners and on whom advice exhortation have no effect, a Corrector, who is not to be a member of the Society, is to be appointed. When reformation is despaired of, and the pupil is likely to become a danger to his fellows, he is to be expelled.

Rules for Professors of Lower Studies

Among the general regulations for the professors of the Lower Studies are those dealing with the method of exposition of a subject or a lesson, and these concerning emulation, in the exposition of a lesson or passage. Four stages are to be distinguished : (1) The whole passage, when not too long, is to be read through; (2) The argument is to be explained, also, when necessary, the connection with what went before; (3) Each sentence is to be read, the obscure points elucidated; the sentences are to be connected together, and the thought made evident; (4) The whole is to be repeated from the begining.

Emulation

Throughout the Constitutions and the Ratio anything likely to excite contention or produce invidious distinctions is deprecated. Graduates are not to occupy special seats in the university classes, and the class lists are to be in alphabetic order. That emulation is not a dominant or integral part of the Jesuit system may be judged from the fact that only four regulations are here devoted to it. It was merely one among other devices to enliven instruction and develop in the pupils a ready command of the knowledge which they had acquired. The directions governing its use state that the concertatio, or contest, is usually so conducted that either the teacher puts the question, and the adversary corrects the answer, or the adversaries question one another. The contest is to be held in the highest regard. It is to take place as frequently as time permits, so that a noble emulation may be fostered, which is a great incitement to study. The contest may be engaged in by one or more on either side, especially by the better pupils of the class against one another. A contest of one against many may even be allowed. An average pupil may sometimes challenge a distinguished pupil. If he overcomes he succeeds to the superior office. Public contests may be allowed on occasion, but only for the better pupils. One class may contend with the class next to it on a common subject of study, both teachers presiding.

The Ratio is not the work of Loyola; it nevertheless represents more fully, and doubtless more justly, his views on, and practices in, education than his Constitutions, in which the subject could be treated only as part of the general work of the society.

Contribution of Jesuits

To the jesuits must be given the credit of providing education with a uniform and universal method. "So far as the evidence of history extends," says crown party, "an organised caste of priests, combining the necessary leisure with the equally necessary continuity of traditions, was at all times indispensable to the beginings of scientific research."[10] The need of a uniform and universal method in teaching was thus declared in the Proam to the 1586 Ratio. "Unless a ready and true method be adopted much labour is spent in gathering but little fruit.... We cannot imagine that we do justice to our functons, or come up to the expectations formed of us, if we do not feed the multitude of youths, in the same way as nurses do, with food dressed up in the best way, for fear they grow up in our schools, without growing up much in learning."[11]

Role of the Teacher

In the selection of teachers something of the same discrimination as Loyola exercised in his choice of the first members of the Society is still demanded. The selected candidates are subjected to a training. Yet the educational authorities in many modern countries have failed to realize the importance of thorough professional training for all engaged in higher education, including university teaching.

Value of Training

The value of training was recognised in the draft Ratio of 1586 in the statement, "It would be most profitable for the schools, if those who are about to be preceptors were privately taken in hand by someone of great experience and for two months or more were practised by him in the method of reading, teaching correcting, writing, and managing a class."

Place of Classics

The predominant place assigned to classics in the jesuit curiculum has historical justification. The Society has not bound itself slavishly to a seventeenth centruy curriculum. The widening of the conception of culture to include not only the classical languages but also a precise use of the mother tongue, an appreciation of modern literature, the principles of mathematics and the methods of natural science, has been recognised by the jesuits. The new subjects, when admitted to the curriculum, have been taught with the same thoroughness as the old.

Successive Teaching

In order of time the mathematical subjects follow the classical subjects. The subjects are taught successively, not simultaneously. On pedagogical grounds the Jesuits defend the successive teaching of different branches of instruction in preference to the simultaneous treatment of a number of subjects. However, they modify this procedure when any government system requires this. Their arrangement is partly recognised in the demand of present day educators who advocate successive periods of 'intensive study' of the various school subjects.

1. Dramatic Method. In retaining the drama as an educational instrument, the Jesuits anticipated the modern movement represented by the dramatic method of teaching history.

2. Direct Method. In insisting on the speaking of Latin they like wise anticipated the direct method of teaching the classics.

3. Repeatition. In repeating the work of the class twice in the year, and thus enabling the abler pupils to spend only half a session in a grade and thus be promoted more rapidly, they introduced a procedure now adopted by some modern school systems.

4. Discipline. The Jesuits' contribution to school discipline was notable. To the early Jesuits we owe the substitution of supervision for compulsion. The principle implied is that prevention is better than cure. They did not, however, dispense with punishment altogether. The Ratio of 1599 recommended the introduction of a Corrector, who was to administer chastisement when such was necessary. The office of Corrector was later dispensed with, but the principle of dissociating punishment from teaching has been retained. Gentleness is especialy enjoined towards the pupils Loyola prescribed as the maxim of the Society that it must always govern by love. That obedience is one of the vows taken by the members of the Society must lighten the work of teaching.

5. Moral and Religious Education. In the Confession and the Communion, the Society possesses powerful instruments for the moral and religious education of the pupil. Through the communion the Society secures practice in worship, an exercise which distinguishes the religious from the moral attitude of life, and a training in which is essential to a complete and generous education.

6. Changing Success. The Jesuit system has survived since its approval by the Pope in 1540. It has adapted itself with a certain measure of success to changing conditions.

7. Universal System. As its exponents are not merely educators but missionaries of a religious faith, it has been applied in almost every country in the world. The Jesuit educational system has taught the world the value of a uniform and universal method in education, and the economy of a cultured and highly trained teaching profession.

Writing of Loyola, Francis Thompson writes, "When he spoke it wast what he said, it was the suppressed heat of personal feeling personal conviction which enkindled men. This has ever been the secret of great teachers, were they only school masters; it is the communication of themselves that avails."[12]

REFERENCES

1. T. Hughes, *Loyola,* p. 99.
2. Francis Thompson, *Saint Ignatius Loyola,* p. 73.
3. *Constitutions,* Pt. IV, Ch. v, 1.
4. *Ibid,* Ch. vi, 4.
5. *Constitutions,* Pt. IV, Ch. vi, 8.
6. *Ibid.*
7. *Ibid.,* Ch. viii.
8. *Ibid.,* Ch. xvii.
9. *Ibid.,* Ch. xii.
10. I. Gomlperz, *Greek Thinkers* (1901), Vol. I, p. 43.
11. *Pachtler,* Vol. V, p. 27.
12. Francis Thompson, *Saint Ignatius Loyola,* p. 181.

13

JOHN LOCKE

(1632-1704)

John Locke was born in a religious family living in an English village in 1632. He was sent to Oxford for his higher education, where he studied philosophy and Greek literature with complete absorption. In 1660 he was presented with an opportunity for demonstrating his scholarship. He was appointed professor of philosophy and Greek literature at Oxford itself, but immediately after a complete change in his life and outlook compelled him to give up this profession. Political philosophy of the day claimed him and he became engrossed in it, so much so that he joined the warring faction, left England and exiled himself in Holland for some time. At this time he was beset with other difficulties as the death of his father forced him to assume all the responsibilities of his family. He returned home from Oxford in order to study medicine but could find no real satisfaction in it. An accidental meeting with Lord Shaftesbury placed him on the post of a secretary which he gratefully accepted. While engaged in this work he revived his intellectual life, and wrote his classic work *Essay Concerning Human Understanding* in 1690. Concerning the composition of this great classic of deductive reasoning and elegant prose it is said that Locke one evening went to an inn for his evening tea. In the course of conversation a question that came up for consideration was how did man gain knowledge of universal truths. Locke made this the subject of his research, and the book consequent upon it gained tremendous importance in philosophical circles.

Locke's own philosophy and his entire knowledge of science have gone into its making. He passed the rest of his days in study and the pursuit of knowledge and breathed his last in 1704.

PUBLISHED WORKS

Collected Works, 1853; *Philosophical Works* edited by St. John in Bohn's Library; *An Essay Concerning Human Understanding* edited by A.C. Fraser, 2 Vols., (1894); *Treatise of Civil Government and A Letter Concerning Toleration*, Charles L. Sherman ed. (1937); *John Locke Selections* edited by M.W. Calkins, (1917); *John Locke Selections* ed. S.P. Lampreche, (1928). Among important works on Locke's philosophy are : I.H.R. Fox Bourne, *Life of Locke*, 2 Vols., 1876; T. Fowler, *Locke*, (1880); A.C. Fraser, *Locke*, (1890); S. Alexander, *Locke*, (1898); M.M. Curits, *Outline of Locke's Ethical Philosophy*, (1890); J. Gibson, *Locke's Theory of Knowledge and Its Historical Relations*, (1917); R.I. Aaron, *John Locke*, (1937); W. Kendall, *John Locke and the Doctrine of Majority Rule*, (1941); C.R. Morris, *Locke, Berkeley, Hume,* (1946).

PHILOSOPHY OF EDUCATION

The publication of Locke's *An Essay Concerning Human Understanding* in 1690 has been said to mark the opening of an epoch in the history of education. It initiated a new era in philosophic thought. His influence on education on the Continent had been considerable.

When resident in Holland and engaged on the great *Essay*, in the latter half of 1684, Locke wrote to his friend Edward Clarke of Chipleigh House in Somerset, giving advice on the upbringing of his friend's children, especially the eldest boy — Edward. These 'Directions' served as the first draft of Locke's *Some Thoughts Concerning Education*. The work, as Locke acknowledges in the concluding paragraphs of the book, does not pretend to be a complete account of the subject of education. But the author hopes that it may give some light to those who venture to consult their own reason in the education of their children rather than wholly rely upon old custom.

Locke did not offer a comprehensive education for all the children of all the people. After being appointed Commissioner of Trade in 1696 Locke drew up a comprehensive plan for making workhouses useful institutions; it included a project for the maintenance and upbringing of pauper children.[1] This provided for working schools to be set up in every parish where such children from three to fourteen years of age would get meals in return for their labour in spinning or knitting. The schools were to be self-supporting. The proposal was not, however, adopted.

Education according to Classes

Locke believed that different classes in the community should have different types of education. He said, "I think a prince, a nobleman, and an ordinary gentleman's son, should have different ways of breeding."[2]

Education of Young Gentleman

Although he makes incidental reference to the education of other classes, Locke's main concern is with 'the breeding of a young gentleman.' Concerning his conception of the ideal gentleman. Locke said, "We cannot but be pleased with an humane, friendly, civil temper wherever we meet it. A mind free and master of itself and all its actions, not low and narrow, not haughty and insolent, not blemished with any great defect is what every one is taken with."[3]

Choice of Governor

About the problem whether a young gentleman should be educated at home under a tutor or sent to a public school, Locke said, "I cannot but prefer breeding of a young gentleman at home in his father's sight under a good governor as much the best and safest way to this great and main end of education when it can be had and is ordered as it should be." Much, of course, depends on the choice of a tutor, and about this Locke said, "The great work of a governor is to fashion the carriage and form the mind to settle in his pupils good habits and principles of virtue and wisdom, to give him little by little a view of mankind and to work him into a love and imitation of what is excellent and praise-worthy, and in the prosecution of it to give him vigour, activity and industry."[4]

Importance of Education

Locke believed that mind is a *tabula rasa*. All minds are identical in structure and the differences found amongst men are the result of education. In the opening sections of the *Thoughts,* he said, "That of all the men we meet with, nine parts of ten are what they are, good or evil, useful or not, by their education. Tis that which makes the great difference in mankind." And he repeated, "That the difference to be found in the manners and abilities of men is owing more to their education than to anything else."[5] Later in the *Thoughts* he qualified his statement averriing "God has stamped certain characters upon men's minds which, like their shapes, may be a little mended, but can hardly be totally altered and transformed into the contrary."[6] In *Of the Conduct of the Understanding* — a work published posthumously — Locke was equally emphatic that there are innate individual differences and that the contribution of education is almost negligible. He said, "Amongst men of equal education there is great inequality of parts."[7]

Role of Formal Training

Formal training is inconsistent with Locke's general empiricist philosophy. It implies the existence of mental faculties. Locke is usually cited as a critic of the faculty hypothesis in psychology, more especially in regard to memory. He said, "Memory is so necessary to all parts and conditions of life, and so little is to be done without it, that we are not to fear it should grow dull and useless for want of exercise, if exercise would make it grow stronger. But I fear this faculty of the mind is not capable of much help and amendment in general by any exercise or endeavour of ours, at least not by that used upon this pretence in Grammar Schools...."

Transfer of Training

Locke rejected transfer of training. In the *Conduct of the*

Understanding, he said, "We see men frequently dexterous and sharp enough in making a bargain who, if you reason with them about matters of religion, appear perfectly stupid."[8] And later he explained, "The mistake is that he is found reasonable if one thing is concluded to be so in all, and to think or say otherwise is thought so unjust an affront, and so senseless a censure, that nobody ventures to do it."[9]

Habit Formation

According to Locke, the practice-effect is specific, not general in habit formation. He said, "The legs of a dancing master and the fingers of a musician fall as it were naturally, without thought or pains, into regular and admirable motions. Bid them change their parts, and they will in vain endeavour to produce like motions in the members not used to them and it will require length of time and long practice to attain the same degree of a like ability."[10]

Utilitarian Criterion

To the question, "To whom should Grammar be taught?" Locke answered, "Men learn languages for the ordinary intercourse of society and communication of thoughts in common life, without any further design in the use of them. And for this purpose the original way of learning a language by conversation not only serves well enough, but is to be preferred as the most expedite, proper and natural. Therefore, to this use of language one may answer that grammar is not necessary. Others there are, the greatest part of whose business in this world is to be done with their tongues and with their pens; and to these it is convenient, if not necessary, that they should speak properly and correctly, whereby they may let their thoughts into other men's minds the more easily, and with the greater impression. Upon this account it is, that any sort of speaking, so as will make him to be understood, is not thought enough for a gentleman. He ought to study grammar amongst the other helps of speaking well.... And to this purpose grammar is necessary; but it is the grammar only of their own proper tongues, and to those only who would take pains in cultivating their language, and in perfecting their styles. There is a third sort of men, who apply themselves to two or three foreign, dead, and (which amongst us are called the) learned languages, make them their study, and pique themselves upon their skill in them. No doubt, those who propose to themselves the learning of any language with this view, and would be critically exact in it, ought carefully to study the grammar of it. Grammar is throughout regarded purely as an instrumental subject and ancillary to language; its formal training value is ignored." Logic and rhetoric are dismissed by Locke on the utilitarian criterion because of the little advantage young people receive from them.[11]

Locke also suggested that there is no transfer between ability in Latin and in English; in Latin "The manner of expressing of one's self is so very different from ours that to be perfect in that would very little improve the purity and facility of his English style."[12]

Values of Mathematics

Locke followed the fashion of his times in regarding mathematical reasoning as the ideal method of attaining truth. In doing so he made admissions which might justify the charge of formal training. He said, "Would you have a man reason well, you must use him to it betimes, exercise his mind in observing the connection of ideas and following them in train. Nothing does this better than Mathematics, which therefore I think should be taught to all those who have the time and opportunity, not to so much to make them mathematicians as to make them reasonable creatures."[13]

In the *Thoughts* Locke maintained that practice in one phase of memory does not result in improvement in other aspects, that the learning of one language may adversely affect the learning of another, and that training in grammar does not improve the mind in general. In the *Conduct of the Understanding* a similar conclusion is deduced in respect of reasoning and of habit formation, though the weight of evidence is against the charge that Locke supports formal training.

Locke's position might be regarded as pragmatic, of which he said, "We shall not have reason to complain of the narrowness of our mind, if we will but employ them about what may be of use to us."[14]

Lock did not assume that man should be omniscient. In the Introduction to the *Essay* he said, "Our business here is not to know all things, but those which concern our conduct." In the *Thoughts* he said, "It is not the tutor's business 'to teach them all that is knowable.' " In his *Essay of Study*, he elaborated, "The extent of knowledge of things knowable is so vast...that the whole time of our life is not enough to acquaint us with all those things, I will not say which are capable of knowing, but which it would not be only convenient but very advantageous to know."

Frequency of Use

In accordance with this view, Locke formulated a principle extensively exploited by modern curriculum makers known as 'frequency of use.' He said, "And since it cannot be hoped he (the pupil) should have time and strength to learn all things, most pains should be taken about that which is most necessary, and that principally looked after which will be of most frequent use to him in the world."

Sound Mind in Sound Body

A sound mind in a sound body is a short but full description of a happy state in this world. "He that hath these two has little more to wish for; and he that wants either of them, will be put little better for anything else." Such were the opening sentences of the *Thoughts*. Locke disposed first of health education, advocating a hardening regime which is the natural lot of the children of the poor. He recommended, "Plenty of open air, exercise and sleep, plain diet, no wine or strong drink, and very little or no physic, not too warm and strict clothing, especially the head and feet kept cold, and the feet often used to cold water and exposed to wet."[15]

Ideal Personality

According to Locke, four things, virtue, wisdom, breeding and learning are necessary in fashioning ideal type of personality.[16]

1. Wisdom. Wisdom is beyond the reach of children since it implies natural good temper, application of mind and experience.[17]

2. Virtue. Of virtue Locke said, "It is virtue, then direct virtue, which is the hard and valuable part to be aimed at in education.... All other considerations and accomplishments should give way and be postponed to this. This is the solid and substantial good (on) which tutors should not only read lectures, and talk of, but the labour and art of education should furnish the mind with, and fasten there, and never cease till the young man had a true relish of it, and placed his strength, his glory, and his pleasure in it."[18] The foundations of virtue are to be laid in religion. "There ought to be imprinted on his mind a true notion of God as of an independent Supreme Being, author and maker of all things, from whom we receive all our good, who loves us, and gives us all things."

3. Breeding. Breeding is largely a matter of right company. Its aim is to secure 'a carriage suitable to his rank.' The rule to be observed here is, "Not to think meanly of ourselves, and not to think meanly of others."[19]

4. Learning. Learning Locke put last. Regarding it as the least part of education, he said, "This may seem strange in the mouth of a bookish man; and this making usually the chief, if not only hustle and stir about children, this being almost that alone which is thought on when people talk of education, makes it the greater paradox."[20]

The explanation that Locke gave in *Thoughts, Concerning Reading and Study* for a gentleman was that "A gentleman's proper calling is the service of his country, and so is most properly concerned in moral and political knowledge; and thus the studies which more immediately belong to his calling are those which treat of virtue and vices, of civil society and the arts of government, and will take in also law and history."

But if the young gentleman is not to remain 'more ignorant than the clerk of our parish,' he must learn to read and write. Various contrivances for learning his letters are described by Locke; after mastering these he is to proceed to reading. After reading comes writing. In dealing with the acquisition of this skill Locke enunciated the principle that if one would do anything well he should not attempt to do two parts of an action at the same time if they can be separated. Learning to hold the pen must accordingly be taught independently of learning to form the letters. Representational drawing is added not for any aesthetic but merely for its practical value.

Place of Languages

In spite of his general pragmatic standpoint Locke did not evade the issue of the place of languages in the education of his pupil. After English, French is proposed. The reason for its priority over Latin is that it is a living language and can be acquired by the direct method. Latin, too, is absolutely necessary to a gentleman. But it should be taught by the direct method and not after the traditional grammatical manner. No man can pass for a scholar who is ignorant of the Greek tongue.

Importance of Mother Tongue

Locke is a convinced believer in 'English for the English.' "Care is to be taken when the boy is learning French and Latin, that his English is not neglected.... since 'tis English that an English gentleman will have constant use of, that is the language he should chiefly cultivate.... I am not here speaking against Greek and Latin; I think they ought to be studied, and the Latin at least understood well by every gentleman. But whatever foreign languages a young man meddles with (and the more he knows the better), that which he should critically study and labour to get a facility, clearness and elegancy to express himself in, should be his own; and to this purpose he should daily be exercised in it."

Curriculum

To complete his curriculum Locke adds arithmetic, astronomy, geometry, geography, chronology, history, ethics, law and natural philosophy. Other accomplishment include dancing and music, and wrestling is preferred to fencing. Locke also recommended a trade. He said, "And yet I cannot forbear to say I would have him learn a trade, a manual trade, nay two or three, but one more particularly.... I should propose one, rather both these, namely, gardening or husbandry in general, and working in wood as a carpenter, joiner or turner, these being fit and healthy recreation for a man of study or business."[21] A young gentleman should learn to keep accounts, "though a science not likely to help a gentleman to get an estate, yet possibly there is not any thing of more use and efficacy to make him preserve the estate he has."[22] Locke regarded seven to fourteen as the best age to acquire the correct accent in foreign languages.

Importance of Method

Locke recognised the importance of method in education. He said., "This I am sure, nothing so much clears a learner's way, helps him so much on it, and makes him go so easy and so far in any inquiry, as a good method. His governor should take pains to make him sensible of this, accustom him to order, and teach him method in all the applications of his thoughts; show him wherein it lies, and the advantages of it; acquaint him with the several sorts of it either from general to particulars, or from particulars to what is more general, exercise him in both of them and make him see in what cases each different method is most proper, and to what ends it best serves." Stating his own general principle Locke said, "He that hath found a way how to keep up a child's spirit easy, active and free, and yet at the same time to restrain him from many things he has a mind to, and to draw him to things that are uneasy to him; he, I say, that knows how to reconcile these seeming contradictions, has, in my opinion, got the true secret of education."

Play-way in Education

Locke anticipated the play-way in education. He said, "Were matters ordered right, learning anything they should be taught might be made as much a recreation to their play as their play is to their learning." A condition of realising this fortunate state of affairs is that the task should be begun at the psychological moment, when the pupil is in the right mood for it, "the favourable seasons of aptitude and inclination be heedfully laid hold of." It should not be prolonged till exhaustion or aversion sets in, "Care should be taken that what is of advantage to them they should always do with delight; and before they are wearied with one they should be timely diverted to some other useful employment."[23]

Role of Teachers

In the course of the task "Masters and teachers should raise no difficulties to their scholars but on the contrary should smooth their way and readily help them forward where they find them stop."[24] As constant attention is one of the hardest tasks that can be required of children, "He that requires their application should endeavour to make what he proposes as grateful and agreeable as possible, at least he ought to take care not to join any displeasing or frightful idea with it." "The great skill of a teacher is to get and keep the attention of his scholar; whilst he has that, he is sure to advance as fast as the learner's abilities will carry him, and without that, all his hustle and bother will be to little or no purpose. To attain this he should make the child comprehend (as much as may be) the usefulness of what he teaches him, and let him see by what he has learnt that he can do something which he could not do before, something which gives him power and real advantage above others who are ignorant of it. To this he should add sweetness in all his instructions, and by a certain tenderness in his whole carriage make the child sensible that he loves him and designs nothing but his good, the only way to beget love in the child which will make him hearten to his lessons and relish what he teaches him."[25]

The aim should be to create in the pupil "a liking and inclination to what you propose to them to be learned and that will engage their industry and application."[26] This, Locke adds, "should be no hard matter if children are handled as they should be. They are to be treated as rational creatures."[27]

Principles of Guidance

Locke was one of the first to express the guidance point of view, "He that is about children should well study their natures and aptitudes and see by often trials what turn they easily take and what becomes them; observe that their native stock is, how it may be improved, and what it is fit for; he should consider what they want, whether they be capable of having it wrought into them by industry and incorporated there by practice, and whether it be worthwhile to endeavour it. For in many cases all that we can do, or should aim at, is to make the best of what nature has given, to prevent the vices and faults to which such a constitution is most inclined, and give it all the advantages it is capable of. Everyone's natural genius should be carried as far as it could, but to attempt the putting another upon him, will be but labour in vain, and what is so plastered on will at best sit untowardly and have always hanging to it the ungracefulness of constraint and affectation."[28]

Discipline

A firm believer in teaching without tears, Locke held advanced views on child discipline. He said, "I am very apt to think that great severity of punishment does but very little good, nay, great harm in education; and I believe it will be found that *alteris paribus* those children who have been most chastised, seldom make the best men."[29] Strongly opposing the use of the rod, Locke said, "The usual lazy and short way by chastisement and the rod which is the only instrument of government that tutors generally know, or ever think of, is the most unfit of any to be used in education."[30] "This sort of correction, naturally breeds an aversion to that which 'tis the tutor's business to create a liking to." If it needs be that offences come, then Locke offered advice suggesting the employment of a Corrector after the manner of the Jesuits, but repeating, "Beating is the worst and therefore the last means to be used in the correction of children and that only in cases of extremity after all gentle ways have been tried and proved unsuccessful."[31]

FEMALE EDUCATION

In a covering letter attached to a fair copy of the early draft of the *Thoughts* sent in 1684 to his friend, Edward Clarke, Locke contemplated dealing with the education of girls, the last sentence running, "Be therefore both you and your lady as severe as may be in examining these rules, doubt as much as you can of every one of them, and when upon a scrupulous review we have settled this part and supplied what possibly you may find wanting, I shall be ready to talk my mind as fully to Madame concerning her daughters, if she continues to be of the mind that may be worth her patience to hear it." And in the *Thoughts* he explained, "I have said he here because the principal aim of my discourse is how a young gentleman should be brought up from his infancy, which in all things will not so perfectly suit the education of daughters though where the difference of sex requires different treatment, 'twill be no hard matter to distinguish."[32]

REFERENCES

1. See R.H. Quick, *Some Thoughts Concerning Education* by John Locke, Appendix A.
2. *Ibid.*, p. 217.
3. *Ibid.*, p. 66
4. *Ibid.*, pp. 88-94.
5. *Ibid.*, p. 32.
6. *Ibid.*, 66.
7. Thomas Fowler, *Locke's Conduct of the Understanding* (Oxford University Press, 1901), p. 2.
8. *Op. cit.*, p. 15.
9. *Ibid.*, p. 20.
10. *Ibid.*, p. 13.
11. *Thoughts*, p. 188.

12. *Ibid.*, p. 172.
13. J. Locke, *Conduct of the Understanding*, p. 20.
14. J. Locke, *Essay Concerning Human Understanding*, Introduction.
15. *Thoughts,* p. 30.
16. *Ibid.*, p. 134.
17. *Ibid.*, p. 140.
18. *Ibid.*, p. 70.
19. *Ibid.*, p. 94.
20. *Ibid.*, p. 147.
21. *Ibid.*, 201, 204.
22. *Ibid.*, 210.
23. *Ibid.*, 108.
24. *Ibid.*, 167.
25. *Ibid.*
26. *Ibid.*, 72.
27. *Ibid.*, 54.
28. *Ibid.*, 66.
29. *Ibid.*, 43.
30. *Ibid.*, 47.
31. *Ibid.*, 83-87.
32. *Ibid.*, 6.

INDEX